CHRISTIAN SEXUALITY

Book design by Laurence Bernier

ILLUSTRATED BY

Shelagh

*Illustrations run consecutively
through the book,
telling a story of their own.*

CHRISTIAN SEXUALITY

A Reflection on Being Christian and Sexual

By

RICHARD R. MICKLEY

A CHI-RHO BOOK
ALPHA-OMEGA PUBLICATIONS

THE UNIVERSAL FELLOWSHIP PRESS
LOS ANGELES

FIRST EDITION
1975

SECOND EDITION

Revised, with Study Guide

TO JOHN

"And let your best be for your friend."

The Prophet
Kahlil Gibran

CONTENTS

ACKNOWLEDGMENTS

For helpful review and suggestions, for his faith in the proposed book, for his endorsement of the finished work, I am grateful to the Rev. Elder Troy D. Perry, Founder and Moderator of the Universal Fellowship of Metropolitan Community Churches, who has brought a new understanding of "Christian sexuality" to tens of thousands of the "heavy laden" all around the world and whose autobiography, *The Lord is My Shepherd and He Knows I'm Gay*, started me on the path that has led to a better life in the Lord's service.

I deeply appreciate the interest of the Rev. Elder James Sandmire, my pastor at the time of writing both the first and second editions, who took the time to read the manuscript and offer valuable help and encouragement. He is the only preacher I have ever known who can consistently preach two excellent sermons every Sunday, fifty-two weeks a year. Needless to say, these sermons have influenced the contents of this book.

I am especially indebted to the Rev. James Glyer, M. Div., Union Theological Seminary, for carefully critiquing the entire manuscript of the first edition and discussing with me changes for the second edition, making many helpful observations regarding theological insights and clarity of expression. Through his efforts and organizational ability, a pilot seminar was held in Los Angeles for which the basic Study Guide materials were prepared. I welcome Rev. Glyer as co-author of the accompanying *Leader's Guide* for group discussions based on this book.

I appreciate the long hours of typing by Jerry Knight and Richard Carr on the manuscript and Marj Anderson in typesetting the footnotes and Study Guide.

How can I express my gratitude to Alan Seifert who devoted his time and talent night after night in a labor of love for the Universal Fellowship in order to typeset the entire book? That was a lot of hours

11

for a nineteen year old to give up. The quality of the work attests to his dedication.

A word about the illustrations is not enough. In May of 1976, Rev. Sandmire preached an extraordinary sermon on a rainbow theme. It inspired many to look for the rainbow in their life. It inspired Shelagh to become a Christian. It also inspired her to create an illustrated booklet on a rainbow theme which she and her spouse Linda subsequently presented to the Universal Fellowship Press for the illustration of this book. Then at my request she designed the cover to continue the same theme. I am really thankful to Shelagh for making this beautiful creation available for this book. I only wish our readers could see the rainbow in full color.

The last work that had to be done was layout and design. I am grateful to Dick Johnson, Director of Publications for MCC Los Angeles, for laying out the individual pages, and to Rev. Larry Bernier for designing and laying out the book.

Finally, I want to thank Miguel for his patience and goodness during the months of writing and final editing during my free time which means I didn't help much around the house or go out much. How can I thank God for him and him for being him for me as a living example of Christian sexuality?

Richard R. Mickley
Mary Ann's Birthday
July 26, 1976

FOREWORD

One of the greatest challenges facing the Christian is the formulation of an attitude concerning morality. No member of the Body of Christ can survive without tools to help form what should constitute God's will for our lives in this area.

The Word of God, the Bible, admonishes:

"Let every person work out their own salvation . . ."

We who are Christians are in a partnership with God, through Jesus Christ, God's Son, once we accept the Christ as Lord, Savior and soon-coming Deliverer.

Jesus came to earth and lived in the same fleshly body that we all dwell in. When he left our earthly race to again dwell with God, the Creator, he made sure that we, the redeemed, had at our disposal tools to help us make judgments concerning sexual morality. God, in offering salvation to all persons, did not plan that people who became Christians should become a group of robot-saints. No, to the contrary, "Those whom God has set free are free indeed!" No wonder the Christian rejoices . . . we are no longer in bondage, but have liberty in Jesus Christ.

This book then is another tool to help us who are called by God to be children of the Divine Realm.

I am pleased that Richard Mickley, the author, asked that I write the foreword for this publication. In working with Richard in the General Headquarters of our Fellowship, I have learned to respect the dedication of this young man. I have watched as he has prayed about, researched, written, and rewritten this manuscript.

Some readers will complain that the answers and conclusions he comes up with are too liberal, and others that they are too conservative. Because they do not seem to indicate a sharp and clear line between acceptable and nonacceptable behavior in the sexual life of the Christian, a few legalists will feel threatened because he has not "majored in minors."

The author speaks for no particular group or organization, but rather shares with you his ideas as a Christian counselor.

I hope that you will read and understand what Richard is saying. And, in a nutshell, it is this: God created sex . . . and it was good . . . and we have a responsibility to use it in a good way.

REVEREND TROY D. PERRY
Moderator, Board of Elders
Universal Fellowship of
Metropolitan Community Churches

AN INTRODUCTION:
THE GENERAL PERSPECTIVE

Christian Sexuality is purposely chosen as the title of this study because it is precisely the subject matter which is considered. At first I hesitated to use this title because I knew some people would react unfavorably to finding these two words side by side.

I could have written a book on being healthy and being Christian, being a good citizen and being Christian, or being fiscally responsible and being Christian, but I have chosen to write on being sexual and being Christian.

I don't see anything wrong with a book dealing with Christian Healthiness, or Christian Citizenship, or Christian Fiscal Responsibility. Nor do I see anything wrong with Christian Sexuality as a fact of life or as a subject for meditation. I see a need for those of us who are human and sexual and Christian to reflect upon responsible and fulfilling ways to put it all together into a meaningful life according to God's will for us.

Therefore, this book explores some of the basic concepts involved in being Christian and some of the basic concepts revolving around being sexual. Then it presents some thoughts on constructing a personal Christian sexuality.

In prayerful meditation I realized this really is a very good reason for facing the subject head-on with a title that says exactly what must be said.

Being Christian calls for a total orientation of the whole created person toward the Creator. Like a compass obeys the pull toward the North Pole, the Christian needs to accept the call to turn toward God. This willing conversion to God causes all of me to go in the same direction. I can't leave behind any aspect of me. I can't turn any part of me in another direction. If I am turning toward God, I can't be like an unwilling bride brooding over what might have been. If I am turning toward God, all of me needs to turn toward God. And all of me includes my sexuality. And this makes it very clear to me that, if I am going to be Christian, I need to explore what it means to live a Christian Sexuality.

*   *   *

This study is title *Christian Sexuality* because it is a study of the sexuality of a fully human, free, and responsible being who has accepted Jesus Christ as Saviour.

This book proceeds from the premise that being sexual is a vital part of being human; that being human is being what God intended when God created us human. Therefore, sexuality, rather than being shunned by the Christian, needs to be explored with openess so that it can be handled with responsibility.

Responsibility is a capability given to human beings that elevates us to a position above all other earthly creatures. Responsibility is a key factor in being Christian. In order to be Christian, I must have the ability to make a response. I must be free to respond to the call to a more abundant life. This is nothing more, nor less, than trying to be what God wants me to be.

I cannot compartmentalize the functioning of my body. "Today I am going to be a breathing person." "Tomorrow I am going to be a heart-beating person." I am a whole person all the time. Therefore, the way I live my life extends to all of me. My response to God includes the way I handle all the components of me.

My response to God as my creator, my redeemer, my sustainer, includes the way I handle my sexuality. I choose to be Christian. All of me is me and all of me is part of my being Christian. Therefore, I have a responsibility to live a Christian sexuality.

*　　*　　*

It should be apparent, then, that this is a Christian meditation book. Its perspective, the way it looks at everything, is from the point of view of "What is Christian?"

I am thoroughly convinced that one's life as a Christian needs to be kept conscious and growing. I also believe that there are three essential elements of a balanced Christian life. These are prayer, study and action. Without a balance of the three, my life as a Christian gets lopsided and wobbles like a tire with a heavy weight on one side. Or if any element is neglected, it falls like a tripod with a leg missing. Or if any leg is too short or too long, the whole thing is dangerously unstable.

This is a meditation book for Christians who want to take a deeper look at the fullness of their Christian commitment.

At the same time, it is written for those who have been too long influenced, confused, and misled into unfulfilled lives because of "theologies" that would separate sexuality from the Creator of sex.

Hopefully this book will offer a new outlook to those who have been led to believe that God is an enemy of sexuality.

It is hoped this book will be a soothing therapy for victims of a paranoia derived from a culture that leaves the impression that "God will get you" if you enjoy your sexuality. This cultural hand-me-down has long since forgotten the difference between responsible sexuality and sex worship. Furthermore, this fear of sex, more than anything else, has imposed a false god on the children of this world. And these children have become the grownups who have passed it on and on to other children of this world. That false god is the "Policeman-In-The-Sky" who stands ready to strike, to punish, and even to destroy if "The Rules are Broken."

I don't have that kind of God. It is my belief that this is not the god of the Christians. This book is written from a perspective that believes in a much different kind of god.

This book had to be written because there are some who dispute the "Christian-ness" of any approach that takes God out of the sky, asserts the essential unity of soul, mind and body, and calls people to a Christian sexuality rather than a shunned sexuality.

The basic perspective of the book, the way it looks at everything, is from the point of view of "What is Christian?"

* * *

The purpose of this book is to offer food for thought to those Christians who want to enter into serious meditation about what it means to be human and sexual and Christian all at the same time.

There is a chapter devoted to each of these topics. Then two additional chapters delve more deeply into what it means to be *Christian* — being *moral* and being *Christ-like*.

I hope this book will be a starting point for those who want to think through a Christian outlook on sexuality.

I hope this book will help some people eliminate sexuality as a stumbling block to spirituality.

I hope this book will get some of its readers started on a regular personal program of prayer and meditation that will lead them into an increasingly conscious life in union with God. I hope for others it will be helpful in their on-going effort to walk with God and bring their sisters and brothers along with them.

One book is not enough for a lifetime of spiritual growth. It is my hope that this book will encourage some people to enter more deeply into a balanced life of prayer, study and action.

Prayer is communication with God, expression of one's love for God, and a way of keeping in touch with God. *Action* is witnessing. It is our effort to bring others to know this GOD who is the center of our lives. We can witness for our God in many ways. We can witness in word by actually

18

telling people of the unbounded love of God and what it has meant on our own life. We can witness in deed. We can feed the hungry, visit the sick, help the prisoners, work for freedom of the oppressed.

But, both prayer and action need to be "fed" by *study*. In this context, study is feeding our mind with the things of God. Study is applying our mind, our thinking, our mental abilities to know God, to know what God wants for human life, to know what God wants from "me." If I want to act as a Christian, I must *know* what a Christian should be and how a Christian should act. My thinking must be Christian.

I began reading lives of the saints when I was quite young. In my high school years, I must have read hundreds of books about people who led holy lives. These dedicated people were role models for me. I wanted to walk with God and talk with God and stay in God's will just as they did.

I don't think we have enough biography of God's servants today. I do see people reading inspiring books. Merlin Carothers is very popular among my friends. His *Prison to Praise* and the follow-up books have an autobiographical flavor. I see my Spanish-speaking friends reading him in Spanish.

We need more of this sort of thing. We cannot grow spiritually unless we feed our minds on the scriptures and the things that pertain to living in a closer union with God.

Childhood Sunday School or catechism will not carry us for a life time. Not if we are serious about being Christian. This book makes no apology about delving into what it means to be Christian. Christianity is life. It is part of the very being of a person. But so is sexuality. Christianity should do something to all aspects of a person's human life. Christianity and sexuality and all other elements of one's life have to be successfully integrated.

In keeping with its title, this book specifically studies what it means to be Christian and sexual and makes no apology for emphasizing what it means "to be Christian."

I hope it will be Christian enough for those who feel the world is all to libertine, and I hope it will be liberating enough for those who feel the "Christian" outlook has been all too oppressive.

*   *   *

It is only fair to forewarn the reader of some additonal elements of the perspective of this book.

First of all, it is Christian as opposed to non-Christian. Its perspective is Christian as distinct from psychological or political or even intellectual. This is not to say that things psychological, political, or intellectual are not or cannot be Christian. All truth is God's truth. What I am saying is that this book will try to keep its focus on what is simultaneously human, sexual, and Christian without taking a stance that is specifically anything other than Christian.

It is more concerned with how a Christian should live than what a Christian should know. It is aimed more at giving the Christian some tips on how to live successfully in the light of the gospel message, than at what one should know in order to be intelligent.

By the same tokens, then, it is more evangelical than theological. It is more interested in the gospel and one's personal relationship with Christ than in any scientific school of the science of God.

It is based on the common experience that human life is a search for that which is beyond, that human personality is never perfected, that a fully alive person is always in the process of becoming. Therefore, this book offers some reflections on the effort of the Christian to perfect one's personality.

I have long been an admirer of Teilhard de Chardin's writings. I think he presents a convincing case for the evolution of the world toward the Omega point, calling for the unification of all people and the perfection of all things in and through Christ.

I hope this book will cause its readers to reflect about how all this fits into their personal life, about how they can progress toward self-realization and become what they choose to become, and about how their own pattern of living is tied to the perfecting of all things in Christ.

This book makes no claim to being an authoritative rule book for the proper conduct of human life. It offers things to think about, rather than rules to follow. It is reflective rather than authoritative.

20

*   *   *

Finally, there are some special approaches I want to mention.

In general I have attempted to avoid technical and theological terms. Even biblical words like "grace" and "saint," and commonly used words like "conscience" and "moral" have widely differing uses and connotations. Even "sex" and "love" mean different things to different people. Definitions are better than ambiguous terms. So I have tried to use definitions for key concepts.

Just as I have tried to avoid technical language for reasons of clarity, I have tried to avoid sexist language for reasons of charity *and* justice. I am appalled at some of the things I wrote less than ten years ago, showing ingrained habits of male chauvenism, a conscience numbed by years of male dominated conditioning. Sometimes it's a real problem what to do with quotations from authors who unconsciously indulged in language which excluded women. "Every man deserves his just reward" says only one thing about women. They are excluded. It is painful to read paragraph after paragraph of non-inclusive language in otherwise good authors. Sometimes, in the interest of avoiding sexism in this book, I have deliberately changed quotations.

Lastly, in the special approach of this book, I am treating heterosexuality and homosexuality as equal variants of human sexual expression. Homosexual love is treated as "normal" on the same terms as heterosexual love. I can only pray that the Christian church will some day absolve homosexuality from sin, as the mental health associations have exonerated it from sickness, and more and more governmental bodies are removing it from the list of felonies.

Neither sin, nor mental health, nor legality, alone or together, form a framework for considering Christian sexuality. Or homosexuality. These factors, in their usual contexts, are peripheral to what this book needs to say about being human, sexual and Christian.

In doing this, I have obtained ideas from many sources, but I have made no effort to stack up authorities for particular ideas as if to prove them. Most "arguments" in the field of

21

religion probably have an equal number of authorities and proofs on all sides (all claiming to be based on the scriptures). This book makes an effort to put together in an orderly manner, from the perspectives already mentioned, some of the thinking that has been done in separate places by various authors on the themes of the focus of this book: the human, the sexual, the moral, the Christian. Consequently perhaps, it should be judged more for its synthesis than for its originality.

* * *

This book, in its first edition has been used by pastors in their counseling and in their pulpits. It has been used by sexual counseling centers as a supplement to their programs. It has been used by individuals around the world for their personal meditation and spiritual growth. It even was the inspiration of a novel which the author graciously dedicated to me.

A Study Guide was developed during a successful six week seminar on *Christian Sexuality*, devoted to discussions of the book, chapter by chapter.

The original outline I prepared contained twelve chapters. As work progressed, I deliberately, and I believe under the guidance of the Holy Spirit, decided to narrow the scope of this book to precisely the subject matter that was most fundamental and most in need of study at this time.

* * *

The objectives of the book are:
1. To present a positive view of what it means to be human so that readers will clearly understand that being human is part of the divine plan of creation and a pre-requisite for being Christian.
2. To depict being sexual as a positive and healthy and normal and good part of being human.
3. To describe being Christian as it embraces being fully and sexually human.
4. To offer guidelines for making moral decisions that will be in line with a truly Christian sexuality.

I cannot guarantee that every reader will discover things they have never heard before. On the other hand, I would offer a word of caution. Not everything may be fully understood on the first reading. We all wear "rose colored glasses" of some kind. What we see through our mind's eyes, we understand with that coloration. A rainy day in Los Angeles is a lot different than a rainy day in Chicago. So, the term "rainy day" is seen through quite different colored glasses by life-long residents of each climate. Not everybody these days agrees with everything Marshal McLuan has written. But, I think he was right when he said we all see the future through our own rear-view mirrors.

Growth, development and fulfillment demand an openness to new ideas. Yet, it is difficult for us to face either the possibility or the necessity of the new. We are comfortable with our familiar ways of looking at things, our old thought patterns, our customary reasons for doing things. But, we have long ago ceased to hope and believe that there might be new ways of thinking, evaluating, relating, even understanding God's revelation to us.

*   *   *

Human beings can develop and become different beings. This may seem quite obvious to some people. It may seem quite ridiculous to other people; but, the sad fact is that most of us never even begin to move in the direction of our possible development. Why? Because most people live their lives in a sort of stupor, not at all aware that they *can* become something different.

Most of those who do recognize the yearning and attraction they have for a different life do not understand that they must want it very much and for a very long time.

People do not know themselves. They do not know what they can become. They do not know what powers and faculties they must develop in order to become something different.

The first thing we have to learn about ourselves is that most of what we *do*, *we* don't do. Most of the things that most of us do, really happen. Almost everything we do is the result of external influences and impacts.

23

That makes us in some sense robots. But, this book is written with a firm faith that human beings do have the capacity to rise above a mechanical existence. The biggest problem is that most people don't know they are automatons or what to do to rise above that level of existence.

I am sure there are many who can point to experiences in their life similar to that mentioned by the Rev. Troy Perry in his autobiography: "At age seventeen I followed the course set out for any Southern young man who decides that he wants to be a man of the cloth. I looked around for the woman who would share my life as a minister's wife. . .I had the impression from our church that you had to marry to be ordained. . .One is pushed toward marriage and having children. . .It was better to marry than to burn. . .That helped me make up my mind to become engaged and to go ahead and marry."[1]

That is one example of how people can become automatons of social pressure. There are a thousand more subtle ways that we are swayed by forces outside of ourselves every day.

The need to rise above this level of existence underlies each chapter of this book. My advice to the reader: if you want to get the most out of this book for your own development, keep a constant awareness of who you are, where you are, and where you are going. As you meditate on each Chapter, ask yourself: who am I as a human being, as a sexual person, and as a Christian? Where am I going as a human being, as a sexual person, and as a Christian?

A STORY

of eventuality .....

Once upon a time there was a bunch of beautiful people

1

To Begin

CONFUSION AND STUMBLING BLOCKS

Jesus is the Light of the world. Bumper stickers and neon signs everywhere proclaim that Jesus is the Answer.

But, still confusion reigns. Even, and especially, among Christians. They want the Answer. They desperately need the Light. They hunger for the abundant life promised by the gospel.

For many, the confusion seems to come because they perceive themselves to be sexual. For many, this somehow has become a block, shading the Light, veiling the Answer, and cutting them off from the abundant Life.

In this chapter, we are going to examine, in a rather sketchy way, some of the stumbling blocks, and see, among other things, how the Christian church itself has shaded the Light.

The author of a 666 page book on sexuality writes that "after a half century of psychiatry, mass education, and apparently shriveling inhibitions, the amount of secret sexual doubt and suffering seems hardly less today than half a century ago, as any psychotherapist knows."[1]

I don't know enough about it to write a 666 page book. I do know that in my years in ministerial work, and in teaching before that, I have encountered hundreds and hundreds, not only of boys and girls, but of men and women, who harbor more than a secret sexual doubt and carry no little bit of suffering along with their doubt and confusion.

The other day a woman in her thirties came into my office. "I'm a charismatic Christian," she began. Then hesitantly she continued, "I just recently accepted the fact that I am gay. I've known it since I was ten. I know I love God, but I want to be sure God loves me. I have to keep rationalizing everything. I want to be comfortable within myself that everything is okay with God and me. If I am rejected by my friends, I can find new friends. But God? Will the Holy Spirit still manifest the gifts now that I have accepted the truth about my identity?"

Where does such a person get answers? Are there answers for every question?

There are many books, some longer, some shorter. Some are liberal; some are conservative. They contradict each other. They add to the confusion.

SOME ANSWERS : MORE QUESTIONS

People are still asking the age old question, "What should I be like in order to be a normal, happy man or woman?" New books are throwing in new questions, such as: "What's normal?" Arno Karlen quotes one psychiatrist's advice-without-an-answer: "Sex without love is a problem, but love without sex is no improvement."[2]

I meet many people who are sincerely trying to live a Christian life. Their questions often go beyond "What is normal and how can I live a happy life?" They want to know: "How can I be a functioning sexual person and a Christian?"

Billy Graham is respected as a spokesperson for the Christian church. He has led millions to a better understanding of the gospel. Can they get the answer from him?

You can hear his eloquent delivery as he holds his open Bible in one hand and points an accusing finger with the other hand. "Sex gluttons are tormented by feelings of remorse. They are saturated with intense strain, unnatural emotions, inner conflicts. . .Personality is thwarted in its search for development. . .Passions are out of control. The end result is frustration."[3]

They hear him speak of the collapse of moral standards. They hear him preach that "it has always been a mark of decaying civilization to become obsessed with sex. . .Moral and spiritual decadence is upon us today. We live in a day when old values are rejected and the sense of purpose has disappeared from many people's lives."[4]

I believe this happens. I believe this is an interpretation of what St. Paul is talking about in the first chapter of his letter to the Romans. "Filthy enjoyments. . .degrading passions. . .monstrous behaviour. . ."

I respect Billy Graham and believe much of what he preaches, but I see two problems:

1. The vast majority of the people in his audiences are not sex gluttons, but have a far different hang-up.
2. And for "Sex gluttons" who do happen to hear his attack, he is using a negative and unconstructive approach.

This book, in contrast, presents a step by step positive presentation of what it means to be human, sexual, and Christian in order to achieve a Christian sexuality.

The first problem is that most of Billy Graham's audience would rather sweep sexuality under the rug and pretend it doesn't exist (especially while they are in church, or with Christians or talking about Christian things.)

Dr. Mary Calderone, the famous sex educator, describes the usual state of affairs from the point of view of young people: "As parents, you have totally failed us. You have not instructed us in the facts about human sexuality and sexual behavior as these facts are documented in studies. Not only have you neglected to teach us these facts yourselves, but you have prevented us from having access to them through others who were willing to teach us. You have been unwilling to learn yourselves, and instead have given us your own biases and opinions as if they were facts. Furthermore, in the face of your unwillingness or inability to give us the facts, you have consistently downgraded sex as if it were something evil or dirty, making us feel that there was something bad about *us* because we experienced what we know are normal

29

sexual thoughts and feelings during childhood and adolescence. How much longer do you think we can respect you if you continue to close off our access to this important area of knowledge?"[5]

Dr. Calderone, of course, was talking about sex education in general, but I think it is equally applicable to a positive presentation of Christian sexuality. I think we can say with Deane Ferm: "The time has come when Christians will have to acknowledge the undeniable existence of sex. This is not an easy task since so many church people have more hang-ups about sex than they do about war and racism."[6]

In addressing the second problem, I affirm there is no way that a Christian can deviate from Paul's teaching in Romans 1. We cannot justify sexual gluttony in the Christian order of things.

At the same time, we have to address the question: has the Christian church helped or hindered people in coming to grips with sexuality? I believe it is because the church has failed that "the overall picture is one of a society more aware than ever of its dissatisfaction, but unable to find satisfying new patterns. . .for it is to sex that we turn for our salvation today. It is our religion. . .sex is the touchstone by which we judge and define ourselves. . .

"Therefore, we believe that if we straighten out our sex lives, sex acts, sex roles, sex relationships, the good life will follow as a matter of course. Conversely, we feel that failure in these things means a failed life.

"Even those who decry the 'cult of sex' often analyze character in terms of sex role, and see one's love life as the test of one's virtue and wisdom."[7]

WHAT ABOUT THE CHRISTIAN?

All this is too shallow for the Christian. It doesn't lead to the Answer. I will try to construct a step by step path through the maze.

First, let us examine briefly the situation in which Christians find themselves as they take up their personal struggle to develop a Christian sexuality.

30

Most of us tend to follow hazy subconscious thought patterns ourselves, such as: Christians want to follow the teachings of Christ. Billy Graham is a respected interpreter of the teachings of Christ. Therefore, I can learn the whole truth of the gospel from Billy Graham.

Christians want to do what is right. Joseph Fletcher, the famous author of *Situation Ethics*,[4] teaches what is right (love and then do what thou wilt). Therefore, I can learn the whole truth of Christian conduct from Joseph Fletcher.

These two thought patterns which lead to more or less opposite answers are both false. They are neither good syllogisms, nor true conclusions. Yet, this is typical of the kind of thinking by which most of us are guided. Neither Graham, nor Fletcher, and I suspect not even Mickley, has all the answers. People don't know how to use the Bible, Graham, or Fletcher to live a happy, healthy, Christian sexual life.

HAS THE CHURCH HELPED?

The issue that has to be faced squarely is stated with tongue in cheek, I suspect, by Sherwin Bailey, the well-known author of *Sexual Ethics*: "Even today there is a popular suspicion that the church is not altogether happy about sex."[9]

Even a superficial look around the Christian church, in both its Protestant and Catholic versions, shows that the church has nearly reached the point of irrelevance in the area of sexuality for millions of people.

We are indebted to Deane Ferm for a few statistics that indicate rather plainly that the church's teachings are falling on many deaf ears.

1. A Gallup Poll indicated that nearly 55% of college students no longer believe virginity is important in the person they marry. Another study revealed that nearly 75% of college students engage in premarital sex.
2. More than a third of the first-born children in the United States are conceived by unmarried parents.
3. Venereal disease is a nationwide epidemic.

4. One of five children conceived in the United States. is terminated by abortion.
5. Living together without marriage is widespread among heterosexual couples.
6. Divorce rates have tripled and at least one in three marriages end in divorce.
7. In spite of traditional views of the structure of the family, half the women of America have jobs outside the home.[10]

We can point to the specific example of the attitude of multitudes of heterosexual Roman Catholics toward their church's teaching regarding birth control. They simply shrug their shoulders and do what they think is right for them. Some have the advantage of the counsel of a wise priest. Some do not. Many leave the church.

Along the same lines, thousands of Roman Catholic priests have tossed off the yoke of celibacy. Some have left the priesthood and married. Others live their private lives in secret (in fear and trembling). Either way, it seems to demonstrate that this discipline is not working as an imposed rule of sexual behavior for the whole profession.

Across the wide spectrum of Christian denominations, hundreds of thousands of gay people have left the church rather than contend further with the Church's oppressive attitude toward people who are homosexual. The other day I received a letter from one of the men I had ministered to in a federal prison. "I am a baptized Catholic. I had the unfortunate experience of being denied absolution by a priest after I told him that I was in love with another man and that we had had sexual relations. I explained that I had loved this man deeply for more than three years, and that our sex had become an expression of our love to each other. I went on to explain that love is a gift of God, and that being of God, love in whatever expression could not be bad. The priest refused my Confession. If I could have found some years ago the solace of the advice you gave me, I probably would never have ended up *here*. I wanted to enter the priesthood when I was young, but the rejection and ridicule I was offered by my

32

church led eventually to my estrangement and embitterment. Surely, surely, we *must* be the children of God. My sexuality is not something I asked for. It is something I grew up with. I always had it. Can I be a sinner without choice? All I ask is love and guidance and your prayers. With much love in Christ, Fred."

In contrast with this, I must tell about a woman who recently came to discuss some questions of sexuality with me. She was a Roman Catholic and quite involved in a small group Christian growth experience. I suggested that she talk with one of the priests from Dignity[10a] in her city. She couldn't believe it when the priest told her: "You did not bring your sexuality on yourself. As you develop a positive sexual relationship, you can grow as a Christian. Remember God loves you. You have a free choice to develop a sinless sexual relationship. But fear sin and avoid abuse. Respect the other. Seek a positive, mutually affirming relationship."

Not all are fortunate enough to find a wise counselor. Abuses are encouraged by the attitude toward sex exhibited by most spokespeople for the churches.

Because the Christian church has not acted sensibly and creatively to apply the Gospel to the people of God today, the church is being ignored by increasing numbers of people. I am not suggesting morality based on majority vote. What I am saying is: if the church does not preach an acceptable sex ethic, the people will form their own, or ignore "ethics" altogether.   —5—

One author sums it up this way: "Whenever society attempts to restrict expression of the sexual drive more severely than the human constitution will stand, one or more of three things must occur:

1) people will ignore the taboos (and do as they choose)
2) or they will turn to perverted forms of sex (such as rape)
3) or they will develop psychoneurotic symptoms (such as compulsiveness).

"The stronger personalities defy the taboos. The weaker ones turn to indirect forms of expression."[11]

Allowing for considerable differences among denominations, it still can be said that the Christian church has held to a rather narrow code of sexual behavior. It appeals to a handed down interpretation of scriptures for its guidelines and expects the government to enforce this code for all citizens. To attest to this, we have laws governing divorce, adultery, bedroom behavior, homosexuality, and even masturbation.

The renowned theologian, Paul Tillich, speaking of morality based on law, says it produces people who are either Pharisees, cynics, or indifferent.[12]

Dr. Norman Pittenger, the world famous theologian, preacher, author, and lecturer, as well as Anglican priest and seminary professor, is convinced that "long years of repression and downright condemnation of sex, not the least in circles associated with the Christian church, are greatly in need of correction by positive discussion."[13]

Unless the Christian church can find new ways of interpreting the Scriptures and making rules for Christians to follow, it should get out of the rule-making business, and give people guidelines for being responsible for their own behavior.

SOME HISTORY

It all started in the strange combination of cultures found in the New Testament world. The situation in that first century after the birth of Christ found the followers of Jesus thoroughly schooled in the teachings of Jewish legalism (laws, laws, and more laws) based on the Old Testament. But at the same time, they found themselves, wherever they went, surrounded by the Roman Empire which had conquered the entire Mediterranean world, encompassing many civilizations, including the "immoral" pagan cultures of the people of Greece and Rome.

St. Paul

St. Paul saw in his travels a pagan world filled with homosexuality, prostitution, and all manner of sexual promiscuity. He tied this all together with worship of false and pagan gods. In the first chapter of his letter to the Christian people at Rome, he speaks of how the pagans refuse to honor the one true God and of what happened to them: *"God gave them up in the lust of their hearts to impurity, to dishonoring their bodies among themselves, because they exchanged the truth about God for a lie and worshipped and served the creature rather than the Creator."* (Romans 1:24-25)

This was the world Paul saw and his views and his writings were influenced by what he observed.

But his world had other weaknesses *that he shared with it.* It was a world that demeaned and dishonored not only bodies, but persons: women and slaves, for example.

Women, created whole persons from the hand of the Creator, found themselves with a somewhat lesser assignment from Paul. *"Woman is for the glory of man. Woman is made for man."* (I Corinthians 11:7-8) *"Wives be subject to your husbands."* (Ephesians 5:22)

In Paul's world, all homosexual acts were associated with pagan idolatry, all women were clearly inferior to men, and slavery was an accepted sociological condition.

Later in this chapter we'll study these three phenomena in more detail.

St. Augustine

As the centuries moved on from Biblical times, other influences re-inforced and strengthened the church's anti-sex and anti-women attitude derived largely from St. Paul.

It is not necessary to trace the whole history of the approach to sexual attitudes in church teachings down through the centuries.[13a] I will only point out a few high points. A great influence was St. Augustine, the great Doctor (teacher of renown) of the Church. In his younger years he indulged in what he later considered excessive sexual gratification. After he became a Christian (and a bishop under the Pope), he entered into celibacy and wrote his *Confessions*, in which he poured out not only his feelings of personal guilt, but his moral philosophy of the sinfulness of the flesh (which he bequeathed to posterity). His moral stance became another cornerstone of church teaching.

To make a long story short, orgasm was, for Augustine, the farthest thing from God. Sexual pleasure was wrong. God created sex for reproduction, *only*. Therefore, pleasure in sex, even in marriage, was to be shunned. For him, restraint or abstinence is the basic rule for morality in sexual behavior. And that set the pace for Christian morality right down to this day. You can picture in your mind's eye: the grimaces and pained looks on the faces of millions of good Christians through the ages who have followed this teaching as they indulged in the "dirty deed" once a year with their spouses, fully clothed, to reproduce. And that picture in your mind's eye would not be fiction.

St. Thomas

In the thirteenth century, St. Thomas Aquinas, another great Doctor of the Church, defined these attitudes with Scholastic acumen and in the sixteenth century they became Catholic doctrine in the Council of Trent. Any sexual act that does not lead to conception is unnatural and, therefore, of course, sinful.

A Church Council, Hitler, and others

Already in the Council of Elvira in the year 305, the church had denied Holy Communion to homosexuals and prostitutes, even on their death bed. By the end of the fourth century, the Christian emperor of Rome had made it the law of the empire that the punishment for homosexuality was burning at the stake. The practice developed that homosexuals, without trial, with only an accuser, were mutilated, tortured, paraded through the streets nude, and burned to death.[14]

The record books of history tell the story of the burning of the faggots. Hitler's massacre of thousands of homosexuals along with Jews and other misfits was not the first or last attack on that sexual minority.[15]

36

Nor is the Christian church alone in its persecution of sexual behavior. On August 1, 1967 (and that is within the lifetime of most readers of this book) 6,000 people watched the execution of a homosexual in the main square of Sana, Yemen. He had been sentenced to death in accordance with Islamic Law which requires: "That a man convicted of homosexuality be thrown from the highest point of the city, but the court said the condemned man could be beheaded instead.

"When the hour of execution arrived, the official executioner did not show up. After waiting twenty minutes, a religious judge asked the condemned man if he would consent to being shot. He nodded and a police officer executed him."[16]

To be sure, many outrages have occured. Many myths about sex have been handed down in all cultures, in all ages. Unfortunately, in all religions and in all churches, church people have all too often been spokespeople for those myths.

Just recently, a book was published by a well known religious group which still proposes, in this day and age, that it is quite possible that masturbation causes more insanity than anything else except intemperance.

MAINTAINING A SANE OUTLOOK

The teachings of Jesus, the letters of Paul, the pronouncements of popes, the writings of religious thinkers, saints and theologians should not be ignored. It is all too tempting to shrug off all "authority," to disregard *all* teachings of those who have misled us in some way.

But, we, too, can make mistakes. We can jump to hasty conclusions. People not trained in all fields of human knowledge can by myopic, seeing only narrow viewpoints.

An example of this may be the hasty plunge of many into use of the "pill." Today, more and more discoveries are pointing to its medical unsafeness as developed to this stage. There was a stampede to use this seemingly safe deterrent to conception before its cancer-producing potential was discovered.

We have to look at all sides. People who administer X-Rays need to take precautions against excessive radiation for themselves while they are using this device to aid in the advancement of health of others.

By the same principles, if sex is demythologized without a Christian perspective, there will be temptations to misuse it. I've seen little children get very sick from eating too much pumpkin pie. I've seen adults misuse beer and horse-racing. It's also quite possible to misuse sex, even while legitimately trying to break loose from the bondage of the past.

The Christian cannot give up Christ because Christ was, in His humanity, a product in some ways of His times. Nor can a Christian give up all morality because in some things, some would-be spokespeople for Christ teach irrational and unacceptable things.

Taking a new look at what it means to be sexual and Christian does not mean that all the old morality can be swept away.

The call for a new look at sexual ethics does not mean that sexual repression should give way to sexual idolatry. Nor is there a place in Christian sexuality for sanctified hedonism.

This book approaches the subject with the understanding that Christ consciousness must triumph over unbridled pleasure seeking. But, I do not agree with Augustine and Aquinas that pleasure is evil. I do agree with Aquinas that human reason should be in control, but I will propose that an educated human reason will control in such a way as to bring about fulfillment.

A NEW RESPONSIBILITY

It should become apparent that a new approach will require a new responsibility. Then some will recognize (hopefully not too late) that it may be far more difficult to deal responsibly with freedom than it would be to follow hard and fast rules imposed by authority. We will try to make it clear that this means it is far more meaningful for my spouse to say to me sincerely and freely, "I love you," than it would be if I stood over my spouse with a club and ordered, "Tell me you love me." Yes, spouses should love their spouses, but it must come from within in resonsible freedom.

The chapter devoted to what it means to be human delves into the freedom that is inherent in being human. The book as a whole deals extensively with the burden responsibility places on the free person.

The freedom we speak of is not unlike the glorious freedom of the children of God of which St. Paul speaks so often. The death and resurrection of Jesus Christ purchased freedom from death, from sin, and from the Old Law. But at the same time, it is precisely a freedom under the new law of Christ, the Law of Love.

THE NEW TESTAMENT : SLAVES, WOMEN, AND. . .

Let us examine, in a closer study, the Law of Love and how it has been applied (or not applied) in three areas where the New Testament is not outspoken in its opposition to oppression.

Let us take a look at some aspects of the New Testament treatment of slaves, of women, of homosexual men and women. Maybe it would be clearer if I were to put it this way: Let's see how the New Testament promulgates justice for people subjected to human bondage, people born female rather than male in a patriarchal society, people who discovered themselves to prefer persons of the same gender in a predominantly heterosexual society.

There are unmistakable sociological factors involved in each of these conditions. The Biblical stance on each of these subjects is influenced by the times of the writer. One can only imagine what might have been the scriptural wording of a commandment against left-handedness if some sociological condition would have made left-handedness appear worthy of stigma.

Slaves

Today, the "church" and society in general have come to a stand on slavery which goes far beyond the stand of either the Old or the New Testament.

I can remember being surprised, perhaps even scandalized, the first time I read the New Testament through all the way. "Slaves *be obedient to your masters.*" I read in Ephesians 6:5-9. I was in high school then. My understanding of Biblical criticism was not very sophisticated. Nor did I have much of an understanding of the far-reaching implications of the social gospel of Jesus. All I could see were the words before me which plainly were *not* condemning the practice of slavery. That shocked me. To me, slavery was immoral, unchristian; yet, the Bible itself takes, at best, a neutral attitude toward it. I remember having a similar shock some years later when it was charged that Pope Pius XII closed his eyes on the mass murders of Jews (and homosexuals) in Nazi concentration camps.

The New Testament does not attack the institution of slavery. Cautious writers of Biblical commentaries are quick to point out that St. Paul neither condemns nor condones the institution of slavery.

Throughout the gospels and the Pauline and Johanine letters, the principle of Christian social reform is clear; the Good News is based on the principle of equality of all. But, when it comes to slavery, it is verbalized in words which express neutrality. The slave need not seek liberty, for all are made free by the liberty purchased by the Lord Jesus Christ. That does not directly address the matter of the bondage of a human slave to a human master.

1. It cannot be denied that St. Paul grants slaves equality with all other human beings in his famous passage in Galatians 3:28, "*There is neither slave nor free; all are one in Christ Jesus.*" But he does not advocate the end of *human bondage*!

2. The implications of the gospel message remain clear. "*He has sent me to proclaim liberty to the captives. . .*" Luke 4:18. The basic principles of Christianity, love and unity (in equality) make slavery alien to the fulfillment of the gospel.

Women

Likewise, the New Testament attitude toward women is today a source of disappointment, if not scandal. I guess it depends on how you look at it. Some writers make a case for the liberal feminism of Jesus in contrast with Peter and Paul.[17]

Many have pointed out the revolutionary aspects of the gospel's Good News. But, when it comes to women, neither the gospels, nor the letters, nor Acts of the Apostles reveal a *revolutionary* attitude. The New Testament does propose principles which should guide Christian conduct and Christian attitude. The message is loud and clear: oppression, both social and legal, is wrong.

Jesus Himself departed from the customs of His time in treating women with love and friendship. His parables often used female figures.

Rachel Conrad Wahlberg in her book, *Jesus According to A Woman*, examines nine parables and lessons of the gospels and shows how they are "woman-affirming" in her mind. "The fact is," she writes, "that Jesus alone among the people of the New Testament did not accept a first century model for women. He alone treated women as whole persons. Whereas Paul and Peter penned extremely repressive passages about women, (scholars). . . are saying that those passages were typical of first century culture and religion, but not (rules) for all times."[18]

The friendship of Jesus with Martha and Mary was genuine. His disregard for convention in his conversation with the Samaritan woman at Jacob's well is a strong indication of His acceptance of women. The Gospels show a complete absence of rejection in His dealings with women.

Yet, there were no women in the twelve apostles and the seventy-two disciples. The fact that there are few women bank presidents today shows the tradition has been continued: keep women in subsidiary positions!

From the beginning women took an active part in the church and seemingly were accepted into full membership. The Acts of the Apostles shows them assisting the male apostles, but not, indeed, preaching and teaching. In fact, they were instructed to keep quiet in the church. This instruction in Timothy 2:11 comes later in the early church and apparently springs from more of Paul's observations of the society around him. Paul saw in Rome some real evils which he perceived to flow from the emancipation of women. He saw a direct relationship between granting equality to women in the Roman Empire and the far-flung moral degeneracy of the empire.

To explain that a little further: Paul saw a genuine authenticity in the traditional solid base of the patriarchal Jewish family life custom. He was theologian enough to recognize the subjection of women was the result of the curse of Eden. But he did not go far enough in verbalizing the theology of redemption. The curse was removed in the saving death of Jesus Christ. The sin of women's subjection to men should be wiped out in the new order of things.

Paul clearly propagandized for the continuation of the put-downs for women. For example, in the matter of prescribing a head covering for women in the worship assembly, Paul bows to the prevailing social custom. It was not proper for respectable women to appear in public with their heads uncovered. Thus, for him, propriety and decency dictate a "law" which freedom in Jesus Christ rightfully makes unnecessary.

"It is obvious that Paul is rationalizing a social custom of which he approves and that in conclusion he resigns himself to the fact that none of his arguments (for this) are fully convincing."[19]

"The Apostle's doctrine that in Christ there is neither male nor female was not taken to mean a programme of political emancipation, which in antiquity *would have been unthinkable*. The social role of women remained that of home-maker and wife. At the same time, Christianity cut across ordinary social patterns more deeply than any other religion, and encouraged the notion of the responsibility of individual moral choice in a way that was quite exceptional."[20]

"Christianity did not give political emancipation to either women or slaves, but it did much to elevate their domestic status by its doctrine that all (people) are created in God's image and all alike are redeemed by Christ. . .Protest against slavery as such came in the fourth century,. . . too little and too late."[21]

Homosexuals

The weakness of Paul's theology as applied to the emancipation of slaves and women can also be ascribed to his theology regarding people of homosexual orientation.

None of us today, neither the ministers, nor the psychologists, and sociologists, nor the gay people know all the answers about the causation of homosexual orientation. Most of the gay people I know *feel* that they were born that way. Not all scientists agree. We do know that the scientists and open-minded theologians of today know more about homosexuality than Paul of Tarsus, the world traveler. In his travels, St. Paul came across all manner of male temple prostitution, phalic worship, and pederasty that he could neither understand nor condone.

I doubt that in any of his missionary journeys in any part of the Mediterreanean world of the Roman Empire where he preached the Good News of Jesus Christ, I doubt that he ever encountered or recognized a love between two men comparable to the love between Jonathan and David. "*Jonathan swore the solemn oath to David because he loved him as his own soul.*" (I Samuel 20:17) "*O, Jonathan, in your death I am stricken, I am desolate for you, Jonathan my brother. Very dear to me you were, your love to me more wonderful than the love of a woman.*" (II Samuel 1:26)

Nor did it, seemingly, occur to him that two women could have a love and concern for each other that was fulfilling for them without the need for any male complement. He was blind, apparently, to the possibility that a Ruth could love a Naomi with all her heart.

43

What I am saying is that homosexual *love* seems to have been unknown to Paul. He simply was not exposed to the *fact*, and the *concept* was inconceivable to him, apparently. Thus, in his mind, homosexuality was only lust, or temple prostitution, or other non-Christian practices which filled his imagination with disgust.

Yet Jesus was silent on the subject.

CAN THE CHURCH CHANGE?

It took the first Christians some time and some "theological debate" to work out a "theology" on circumcision and a number of other practices that relate to their milieu. On most of these subjects, Jesus was silent. In Acts 15:28, we read of the decision of the Apostles gathered at the council of Jerusalem that circumcision is not necessary for gentile converts.

It took longer for the Christian church to work out its stand on the enslavement of human beings and the subjection of women to "their husbands" and to males in general — a theology that is far from worked out to this date. The longest standing situation of foot-dragging is in working out a theology of justice toward those whose affectional orientation is toward those of the same gender.

Paradoxical as it seems, however, Paul put the principal emphasis of his teaching on love (as did Jesus before him and John writing after him). "In general, Paul and other early Christians accepted the moral commands of the Old Testament and the best standards of Jewish and pagan ethics, even as they claimed theoretical freedom from all external rules."[22]

The only thing that seems to be clear is that the basic ethical standard was the law of love, and it is possible to argue that "Jesus tested the Old Testament law by what was really love to God and neighbor, but his teaching regarding the law is hard to reconstruct. . ."[23]

I am pointing out these developments in Christian theology as a precedent for a long overdue development in Christian attitude toward homosexual love. *If the Christian community can develop a theology of justice toward slaves*

-8-

44

and women, is there any good reason why the Christian community cannot apply the same principles of the Law of Love to another segment of the human race, those rejected because they perceive themselves in a minority position due to their love-object orientation?

It is not surprising to me that Jesus and Paul seemed to conform to the customs of their day in their attitude toward women. It is not surprising to me that the attitudes of Paul toward Greco-Roman moral degradation should strongly influence his teachings on sex and marriage.

THE CHRISTIAN'S CHOICE

What I am saying is that intelligent people who want to be Christian are faced with some choices. It could mean rejection of Jesus and Paul and, of course, Christianity. Many have chosen that way out.

It could mean remaining Christian and taking the following stands:

1. Feminism is wrong; equal rights for women is an un-Christian concept.
2. Homosexual love is wrong. Homosexuals cannot be Christians.
3. Sex is for pro-creation only. Anyone who deviates from this concept over a long period of time cannot be Christian.
4. Slavery is okay; it's not condemned by the Bible.

Another alternative is to find a new and valid way of interpreting what it means to be Christian.

I think we need to take a look at where Jesus and Paul were coming from — and what that means when translated into twentieth century conduct.

I am concerned about the fact that negative attitudes became so strongly entrenched that they have been basic rules for Christian living right down to our present time. The church was able to throw off eventually its allegiance to human slavery, even to the extent that it was condoned in the New Testament. But its attitude toward

45

sex-not-for-procreation, toward love of people of the same sex, and toward equality for women have persisted. The on-going debate in the Episcopal Church over the ordination of women is a symbol of at least that church's attitude toward women. The matter is surfacing and heading for confrontation in the Roman Catholic church. Many major denominations have begun to discuss questions relating to justice for homosexuals. In most cases, however, they are only dealing with peripheral issues such as "equal rights to employment, and housing," but hardly equal rights to the Kingdom of Heaven for people who are practicing homosexual love instead of heterosexual love.

CHANGE

"Perceptions must change first — and this is happening. Then attitudes change, and this is happening. Then actions begin to change. And this, too, is beginning to happen. I see a shift of consciousness resulting in affirmative action in many areas of church and society."[24] Rachel Wahlberg is speaking of women's liberation, but I think the perceptive reader can apply the same statements to gay liberation.

"A theology of women is beginning to emerge, a recognition that doctrine and structure and concepts of ministry have been based on theological attitudes dating back to patriarchal concepts of male superiority and female subjection."[25] Or one could say, "dating back to exclusively heterosexual thought patterns and concepts of human relating. . ."

"Church teaching and preaching must reflect Jesus' affirmation of women, deliberately rejecting the historic association of women with sexual sin which has resulted in anti-women interpretations of the past. To balance nineteen centuries of Christian dogma interpreted from the male point of view, women writers, professors, and theologians are needed to balance out negative attitudes concerning women which pervade major Christian thinkers from Paul and Augustine to the present. " 26

46

Simultaneously, church teaching and preaching must reflect Jesus' affirmation of *all people*, deliberately rejecting the historic association of homosexual love with lust, temple prostitution, and phalic worship which has resulted in anti-homosexual interpretations in the past. To balance nineteen centuries of Christian dogma interpreted from the 'heterosexual-only' point of view, homosexual writers, professors, and theologians are needed to balance out negative attitudes concerning homosexual men and women which pervade major Christian thinkers from Paul and Augustine to the present.

LIBERATION

"If we are not all liberated in Christ, then no one is liberated. It is imperative that all free-spirited women and men insist that the church carry out its true freedom in the gospel by dispelling at all levels, — and in all its segments, doctrines, hierarchies, interpretation and preaching — any vestiges of discrimination against any group of people. . . The goal of Christians is to be neither Greek nor Jew, neither slave nor free, neither male nor female, (neither heterosexual nor homosexual), but full persons doing the work of Jesus Christ."[27]

The Rev. Freda Smith, a pastor and Elder in the Universal Fellowship of Metropolitan Community Churches, wrote in 1973, "Liberation is not changing the sex of the person who is on top. It is necessary to establish dialog between the sexes where we deal realistically with the situation as it stands, and the direction we are going."[28] –9–

Three years later, Rev. James Sandmire, pastor and Elder in the Universal Fellowship, delivered a sermon on the subject of women's liberation in the church. "I don't believe," he declared, "we must be inevitably heading for disaster over this issue. In the recent history of our Fellowship the increasing numbers and importance of women in our congregations have led to broad concern and dialog on the place of the women's liberation movement within the church. Difficult questions about sexism, hierarchical church organization, women in the ministry, de-gendering hymns and –10–

scriptures have surfaced. . .We need men who understand that women's liberation is really human liberation. . .We need creative women who can help address concerns in a way that clearly benefits all."[29]

Letty Russell in her excellent book, *Human Liberation in a Feminist Perspective — A Theology*, gives a clear definition of liberation theology: "Liberation theology is an attempt to reflect upon the experience of oppression and our actions for the new creation of a more human society. . . It is concerned with the liberation of all people to become full participants in human society."[30]

Dr. Lewis Maddocks, Director of the Council for Christian Social Action, United Church of Christ, concluded his article, "The Law and the Church vs. the Homosexual," in the excellent book, *The Same Sex*, with this list of recommendations to the Christian Church:

1. Speak out in support of repeal of laws which make criminal, homosexual practices between consenting adults in private.
2. Support a change in the present policies of complete exclusion of homosexuals from federal employment, from induction or enlistment into the armed forces, and from holding security clearances.
3. Oppose, where they exist, police policies of entrapment in the enforcement of laws against solicitation by homosexuals.
4. Admit homosexuals, as such, fully into the life and membership of the church.
5. Cease whatever discrimination exists against homosexuals, per se, in admission to seminaries, in ordination, and in employment as national, conference, and local church staff."[31]

I cannot conclude this section without at least a brief statement from Dr. Robert L. Treese, a United Methodist minister who is a professor of theology at Boston University. "The homosexual, no less than the heterosexual, needs understanding and sympathetic pastoral guidance in the struggle for ethical fulfillment. The homosexual, no less than the heterosexual, needs the spiritual and emotional support of a church which enables redemptive relationships to occur.

48

These needs are largely unfulfilled at the present time. It is crucial that we concern ourselves with them in the immediate future. The rapid emergence of the Metropolitan Community Church as a national movement of Christian gay people can, in this context, only be seen as a judgement on the church and on the church's outdated and painfully inadequate understanding of this aspect of human sexuality."[32]

FROM REJECTION TO THE ANSWER

Borrowing a thought from MCC pastor, Howard Wells, we can say that rejected people — blacks, other minorities, women, gay people, the young, the elderly, people in any kind of bondage, the handicapped, institutionalized people — can and must find Christ through the aspect of themselves rejected by the world and thereby find their identity.[33]

In the acceptance of our humanity and its rejected aspects, we find Christ. And that brings us to the next chapter, the study of what it means to be human.

Progressively we shall talk about what it means to be human, what it means to be sexual, what it means to be Christian, and what it means to be moral so that we can live a Christian sexuality.

STUDY GUIDE: INTRODUCTION

The study questions provided at the end of each chapter of this book are intended for use in Christian Education classes, discussion groups, and specific seminars based on this book.

A Leaders Guide is available from the publisher of this book. The questions are provided here in order to have them available for all participants without the necessity of further reproduction.

The questions given in this edition are, for the most part, those developed by Rev. James Glyer and Rev. Richard Mickley working with a team of twenty-six leaders in Los Angeles during a pilot seminar of six weeks in length. One two hour session was devoted to each chapter.

From the very beginning it was evident that two hours was not enough to have a full discussion of more than three or four questions. Yet, each chapter raises dozens of questions which can be profitably discussed.

For this reason, the study guide contains a variety of questions. This makes it possible 1) for the discussion leader in a two hour session to choose questions of interest at that time, 2) for groups, such as general Christian education programs or lay minister training classes, to devote more than two hours to the discussion of each chapter, and 3) for the correspondence course lessons to utilize the questions printed in the book for some of its study guide material.

BASIC GUIDE FOR A SEMINAR

The following basic seminar guide is provided, although a more detailed Leaders Guide is available.

The leaders meet for two sessions of two hours each for training prior to the first session of the seminar. This might be done in the same time slot for two weeks before the seminar begins.

The six weeks seminar has six two hour sessions. A general guide for each session might be as follows.

1. All participants assemble together.

2. 10 minutes. Brief introduction of the chapter. Perhaps using the outline provided at the beginning of the study section, perhaps a reading of several thought provoking paragraphs. The object of this is to focus attention of the participants on the subject matter of the session.

3. The participants are assigned to discussion leaders in groups of four to six. The discussion leader takes his or her group to the assigned place.

4. In the group:

    a. 5 minutes. Opening exercise (some sort of get acquainted

sharing or "warm up" in which everybody participates.)
   b. 60-70 minutes. Discuss selected questions, perhaps two selected by the leader, others selected by participants.

   5. 20 minutes. Return to full group and share insights. "We discussed question _____ and this was our observation. We found this _____ particularly interesting about discussion of question _____ ." (Some groups prefer to eliminate this and spend the extra time in the small group.)

   6. Leaders complete evaluation sheet and note the comments from the group that would answer question 5 above.

   7. 15 minutes. Leaders meet for report and evaluation at conclusion of session. Plan next session. This short meeting is very important.

REVIEW OF CHAPTER 1

Jesus is the answer, but confusion reigns. Sex seems to be a stumbling block. And the church has been a part of the problem.

People want to know how they can be sexual and Christian. Billy Graham preaches against sex gluttons. We agree, but feel sex gluttons don't hear him, and the people who do hear him are people who would rather sweep sexuality under a rug.

The Christian church has nearly reached irrelevance for millions of people. Statistics show traditional church teachings on sexual behavior are being ignored by many.

Trends in church teachings on sexuality started with St. Paul who was influenced by the times and environment he lived in. St. Augustine preached the sinfulness of the flesh and passed that philosophy on to all of Christendom.

St. Thomas defined that the goodness of sex lies only in procreation. Homosexuals through the centuries were tortured and burned at the stake and massacred by the thousands by Hitler.

Even though abuses have abounded, Christians cannot blame God for it, and give up all morality. Christians are set free by the death and resurrection of Jesus Christ and that places on them a tremendous responsibility.

The church has progressed beyond the New Testament tolerance of slavery. The church is coming to see the immorality of the oppression of women. Is there any good reason why the Christian community cannot apply the same principles of the law of love to homosexuals?

If we are not all liberated in Christ, then no one is liberated. Liberation is not changing the sex of the person who is on top. We need to understand that women's liberation is really human liberation.

In the acceptance of our humanity and its rejected aspects, we find Christ.

51

STUDY QUESTIONS – CHAPTER 1

(The question number is printed in the margin, beginning at the beginning of the chapter.)

1. Is this question a common occurence? "I know I love God. But does God love me?" Have you ever been in this situation, or known anybody who felt this way?

2. Does Billy Graham paint a realistic picture? Do you think his approach stops the "sex gluttons"? Do you think it solves the "sweep it under rug" hang-up?

3. What does Deane Ferm mean when he says church people have more hang-ups about sex than they do about war and racism?

4. What is the purpose of quoting these statistics?

5. In what way does this statement seem to be true (or untrue to you): If the church does not preach an acceptable sex ethic, the people will form their own.

6. What is the difference between 1) the church making rules and 2) giving the people guidelines for responsible behavior?

7. How can it be more difficult to deal responsibly with freedom than to follow rules imposed by authority?

8. What is your understanding of the New Testament teaching on slaves, on women, on homosexuals? What is the author trying to bring out by this brief study of these three sociological conditions? Is this study beneficial to you in seeing how the theology of the church can change?

9. What does Freda Smith mean when she says liberation is not changing the sex of the person who is on top?

10. What does James Sandmire mean when he says, "women's liberation is really human liberation"?

11. What does Dr. Treese mean when he says the emergence of the Metropolitan Community Church can be seen as a judgment on the church?

12. Close the discussion by each person in the group summarizing what the chapter meant to him or her. Perhaps you could base your answer on some of the points listed in the outline of the chapter above.

CONCLUDE

Give each person an opportunity to offer a sentence prayer of thanksgiving for something suggested by the discussion and one petition brought to mind by the discussion.

and because they were thought of as .... different

they often experienced pressures from Society

which involuntarily made them become ugly on the inside

2

To Be Human

THE MEANING OF HUMAN LIFE

To be human is to be as God intended when God created human life.

To be fully human is to use effectively all the special gifts given to humanity.

To ask what it is *to be human* is to ask what is the meaning of human life.

To know what it is to be human is to know what makes a human being *human* as opposed to less than human.

I remember a couple of years ago when I was writing another book. I sent the manuscript for critique to a good friend, a very religious man of deep religious insights. But, he had grown up in the "school" that considered the world and the flesh equal to the devil as enemies of God (and people) and that somehow being human was a curse that could be overcome by fasting and self-flagellation. So, when he found in my manuscript some helps to becoming "more human," he wrote back to me, "I thought that is what we are trying to get away from!"

Let me make it very clear from the beginning. That's not what we are trying to get away from. I am devoting a full chapter to the definition of what it means to be human, trying very hard to show that we should try to be what God intended us to be when God gave us the gifts of humanity.

Human Life is Different

To know what it is to be human is to know what makes this particular bi-ped different from all other creatures.

Human beings are bi-peds. Birds are bi-peds, of sorts. What makes a bird a bird and a human being a human being?

Gifts

Aside from the obvious differences of the two species, there are extremely important differences. Human beings have gifts of intelligence, will, and freedom that no other bodily creatures have.

Birds can fly. Does that make them higher than human beings? Of course not. But, the unfortunate thing is that rarely do human beings know the heights to which they have fallen heir, the heights they can achieve.

Jonathan Livingston Seagull really wasn't a seagull at all. He is a symbol of the heights to which human beings can aspire.[1]

In the beautiful transactional analysis book, *Born to Win*, there is a meaningful story I have used in sermons. Again it is a story about a bird which is really a parable for us. Let's call it the Parable of the Eagle: Be what you can be.

The Parable of the Eagle

"Once upon a time, while walking through the forest, a certain man found a young eagle. He took it home and put it in his barnyard where it soon learned to eat chicken feed and to behave as chickens behave.

"One day a naturalist who was passing by inquired of the owner why it was that an eagle, the king of all birds, should be confined to live in the barnyard with the chickens.

" 'Since I have given it chicken feed and trained it to be a chicken, it has never learned to fly,' replied the owner. 'It behaves as chickens behave, so it is no longer an eagle.'

" 'Still,' the naturalist insisted, 'it has the heart of an eagle and can surely be taught to fly.'

"After talking it over, the two men agreed to find out whether this was possible. Gently the naturalist took the eagle in his arms and said, 'You belong to the sky and not to the earth. Stretch forth your wings and fly.'

"The eagle however, was confused. He did not know who he was, and, seeing the chickens eating their food, he jumped down to be with them again.

"Undismayed, the naturalist took the eagle on the following day, up on the roof of the house, and urged him again, saying, 'You are an eagle. Stretch forth your wings and fly.' But, the eagle was afraid of his unknown self and world and jumped down once more for the chicken food.

"On the third day the naturalist rose early and took the eagle out of the barnyard to a high mountain. There, he held the king of the birds high above him and encouraged him again, saying, 'You are an eagle. You belong to the sky as well as to the earth. Stretch forth your wings and fly.'

"The eagle looked around, back toward the barnyard and up to the sky. Still he did not fly. Then the naturalist lifted him straight toward the sun and it happened that the eagle began to tremble. Slowly he stretched his wings. At last, with a triumphant cry, he soared away into the heavens.

"It may be that the eagle still remembers the chickens with nostalgia. It may even be that he occasionally revisits the barnyard. But as far as anyone knows, he has never returned to lead the life of a chicken. He was an eagle though he had been kept and tamed as a chicken.

"Just like the eagle, people who have learned to think of themselves as something that they aren't can re-decide in favor of their real potential."[2]

-2-

A Sense of Destiny

Human beings can think. Perhaps the most important thing they can think about is the meaning of life. Certainly there is no other inhabitant of earth which can ponder the mystery of its own origin and ultimate destiny.

-1-

Ants have amazing skills. They accomplish almost unbelieveable wonders in the world by working together in such an organized way that if it were a human project with human laborers, it would take a whole hierarchy of highly trained personnel, skilled in personnel management techniques, to hold it all together.

Yet, there does not seem to be any indication that ants, with all their instinctual skills, have any sense of destiny beyond the here and now.

Purpose

Human beings worthy of the name will find on their mind often the question: "Why am I on this earth?" The thoughtful person will ponder: "For what have I come into existence?" Not satisfied with questions of one's origin and earthly life, the thinking person will ask: "Does it all end when my breathing stops, my heart no longer pumps, and my brain ceases to function?"

How does one assure a dying person that life had a purpose? Even if that person left behind unique products of his or her personal work or talent, immortal works of art, and passed on great knowledge and love to those who live on, can you assure that person that life had a purpose? If the unique person is blotted out completely in death, how can the purpose of its existence be completely fulfilled?[3]

Contrast

There is no doubt in my mind that human beings can reflect upon where they came from and where they are going — and that animals can't. However, I don't see any need here to present a full scientific study contrasting what is purely animal and distinctly human. The thrust of this chapter will be to present reflections on some of the characteristics which make human beings human. The contrast with other beings will be evident.

But more importantly, it will be constantly implied, if not emphasized, that human beings are not really human, or not fully human anyway, if they are not at least striving to use the special gifts of humanity in conducting their lives.

How often have we heard of a person languishing in a hospital bed for months, unconscious after an accident. Somebody inevitably says without intending to hurt that person or persons close, "She's just a vegetable." This is not complimentary, but it's not a put-down, either, in the case of the accident victim who cannot exercise the human powers of intelligence, will, and freedom.

In the United States, a high court ruled that support systems which had been artificially sustaining life could be removed from a person unable to function above the vegetable level.[4]

This court decision is almost equivalent to saying a human life is not really a human life if it is incapable of functioning above the vegetable level.

But what about the talking, breathing, eating persons we see walking around us, sometimes in our shoes, whose life is hardly distinguishable for its humanity?

Choice

Animals have senses, but not the ability to choose and act for a pupose. Human beings can choose *this* or *that*, *because* of a reason they believe makes their choice reasonable. The choices of animals are really reactions determined by stimuli and reflexes. That means they really don't have the gift of freedom.

Animals:

feel hunger	—	look for food
see food	—	eat food
have sex urge	—	seek sex release

Human beings have the ability to decide if and when and how they should look for food, eat food, or have sexual release.

Human beings can consciously survey and consider everything, even their thought. Human beings are a thinking, conscious, responsive part of creation that in growing freedom and choose the good.[5]

CREATION

In studying what it means to be human, creation is a starting point that should not be ignored. The Christian perspective must include a great respect for creation and within creation a particular reverence for human life, including our own life and our own humanity.

The beauty of the Genesis story is the way it brings out the essential goodness of all creation. God created all things good. Nothing God created was evil. "And there is one God whose creation is good. There is no other god who created evil things. Evil came from human beings abusing their God-given freedom."[9]

Whether I believe in evolution or the instantaneous creation of human beings, the important thing is to understand what Genesis is really telling us. A better understanding of the Bible, of Biblical criticism does not discredit Genesis (or God or the Word of God). It helps us to learn what is most important in the creation narrative(s). Included in that highly important message is the revelation that God brought all things into existence, that all things were created good from the Word of God, that God had a special purpose for bringing human beings into existence, and that God poured out love on human beings in a special way.

In the Image of God

The creation story in Genesis I also teaches that human beings are created by God in the "image and likeness" of God. In one of the most stimulating chapters in a totally to-the-point book, *Our Faith*, Emil Brunner paints a poignant word picture of the mystery of life. I am going to share just a portion of it here.

First, Brunner uniquely describes *how* God created human beings. He says we are what we are because God made us so. We have received our life, our existence, our peculiar being from God. Whether or not, he theologizes, God has employed an evolution of millions of years for the purpose of creating human life is the critical concern of the natural scientist. "When I say God creates human persons, I do not deny that people orginate from earthly parents. God uses human parents to create human being."[7]

He goes on to explain what it means that God created human beings in God's own image. It is only of human beings that this statement is made. That we are made in the image of God distinguishes us from all other creatures and somehow makes us similar to God. For what is it that is expressed by this word "image" but similarity of some sort? What distinguishes human beings from the rest of creation is the share we have in God's thought. We have the gift of "reason" as distinguished from mere perception. We can think into the eternal and infinite.

Brunner says, "we are not simply human beings as foxes are foxes. But we are *human* beings only when God's word has an echo in us. God says I am your God."[8] A really human person will respond, "Amen. You are my God." God says, "You are mine." A really human person will say, "Yes, Lord, I am thine." That means we are human creatures to the extent that we let the creator speak to us. We are human beings only to the extent that we let God's word echo in our heart. To the degree that this fails to happen we are inhuman.

No fox behaves "unnaturally" because a fox comes finished from the work of God. Foxes do foxy things, do foxy things, do foxy things.

But, human beings can say yes or no to God, to God's plan, to all the things God destined as the goal of this creative act.

In the yes or no, human beings become either human or inhuman. The freedom to say yes or no to God is the mystery of humanity.

"We have this freedom from God because God has addressed us. Were God to stop speaking to us, we could answer no more, either yes or no. We would then have ceased to be human beings. It is in this way God desires to have an image: people who love the God who first loved them, who reply to the creator who first addressed them."[9]

In studying what it means to be human as quite distinct from what it is to be sub-human, we would do well to keep in mind what it means *to be made in the image and likeness of God.*

God has given human beings many special gifts not bestowed on other creatures. In the following paragraphs we will reflect on some of the special gifts which are marks of authentic humanity — if accepted and used.

SPECIAL GIFTS

As we reflect on these special gifts, it would be helpful to remember what we said in the introduction. None of us comes any ways close to living up to our potential as human beings. Consider the following questions posed by Professor Ouspensky:[10]

1. What does it mean that human beings must become different?
2. What does different mean?
3. What inner qualities and features can be developed and how can this be done?
4. Why can't all people develop and become different beings?

He devotes his whole book, *The Psychology of Man's Possible Evolution*, to answering these questions. In short, "The answer is very simple," he says. "It is because they do not want it. It is because they do not know about it and will not understand without a long preparation. The chief idea is that in order to become a different being a person must want it very much and for a very long time."[11]

Professor Ouspensky goes on to devote his excellent book to applications of his theory of human psychology which go far beyond the scope of this book. But the questions and comments quoted here are valid and very important to keep in mind for it is true that we must "acquire qualities which we think we already possess, but about which we deceive ourselves."[12]

Authentic Humanity

The marks of authentic humanity which we shall study first are:

> *primacy of the spirit
> *an awareness of self
> *freedom
> *ability to make value judgments
> *power to love
> *ability to experience joy
> *communion with others

Primacy of the Spirit

In Christian thinking, the spirit is the higher power, the human faculty most like the divine. Paul, John, and the Synoptic authors use the term spirit in a wide variety of ways. Perhaps in an over-simplification, we can settle on the use of the term in Galatians 5:17 which indicates that the spirit is the principle of eternal life.

I have always enjoyed reading the seventh and eighth chapters of the Book of Romans in the same sitting. The contrast between the flesh and the spirit is brought out here in a really dramatic way. Chapter seven recounts the inner struggle, the powerlessness of a person trying to fight the fight alone, Chapter eight shows the strength that comes from living in the spirit.

"I fail to carry out the things I want to do. I find myself doing the things I hate. . .Instead of doing the good things I want to do, I carry out the sinful things I do not want. . . This is my unspiritual self." (Paraphrase from Chapter 7)

"It is death to limit oneself to the unspiritual. Life and peace can only come with concern for the spiritual." (Romans 8:6)

It can be said that where the spirit is in control, there a truly human life is lived. The spiritual principle in human life gives meaning and purpose and existence beyond the material, beyond the corporeal, beyond the plant and animal.

To the extent that a person is guided by instinct, human life is reduced to less than its potential. An authentic human life, however, is not one where all instinct, emotion, or weakness is absent, but one where the higher power, the spiritual aspect of a person is in control.

It is a special gift of humanity to be able to make this choice: flesh or spirit. This does not say the flesh is necessarily evil. It says human beings have a special power: the ability to put the spirit in control of one's life.

– 4 –

This happens when we recognize that we are weak, but God is strong. We can put the spirit in control, because *"if Christ is in you, then your spirit is life itself. . .through his spirit living in you."* (Romans 8:9-11)

Self Awareness

Self awareness is a special characteristic of authentic human living. The human person is aware that "I am hungry." "I am eating." Not just my stomach is hungry and my hands and mouth are feeding it. I am aware of my wholeness.

This awareness of the whole person is a power not granted other creatures. It can be safely said that without some genuine self awareness, no one could live humanly.[13]

Self awareness is the gift by which one is aware of the vitality of one's senses, emotions, intellect, and will.

But to be aware of oneself, one must begin to know oneself, a proposition as old as Socrates. Professor Ouspensky says we do know what it means to know ourselves. Therefore, I conclude that is why we do not know what it is to be fully aware of ourselves, and thus to be fully human.

Ouspensky says we can start with self observation. It is not enough to know our desires, tastes, capacities, and intentions. We must study also how we function automatically in so many areas. We will observe that much of our time is spent in states of less than full consciousness.[14]

By self study, we can become aware of sides of ourselves which can become more conscious and other sides which are harmfully mechanical and must be eliminated.

He describes four manifestations which particularly drag a person down. They are particularly hard to observe in oneself, he explains, and therefore to overcome. In the terminology of this book, these are some of the things that keep a person from advancing to a fully human manner of living.

The four manifestations are:

Lying: speaking of things one does not know as though one knows and can know;

Imagination;

The expression of negative emotions: depression, self pity, fear, jealousy, anger, etc.;

Excessive talking: unresisted talking makes it impossible to observe anything.[15]

If a person is able to observe these manifestations within oneself, then it is possible to begin to know one's utter mechanicalness a great deal of the time.

I mention these manifestations here, first of all, to show that human beings are the only beings on earth capable of self awareness and self observation and thus capable of overcoming lying, imagination, negative emotions, talking. Yet, even in people who have this power a full reaching of their human potential is extremely rare, if not impossible. I feel this is worth pointing out because you and I tend to slide through life without any effort to use our gift of self awareness to rise above the level of sleep walking, to reach upwards and outwards in the direction of our potential.

Self awareness is a gift by which our intellect and will can be alive and searching. The fully functioning, fully human person (impossible as that is in the context we have described above) is not only aware of physical, psychological, and spiritual hungers and activities, but accepts them as good under the control of the spirit.

Such people can be at home with their body, with their emotions, impulses, thoughts, and desires. They can be open to new sensations, emotions, and changing thoughts and desires.

All this is part of the special mark of humanity, the ability to be aware of oneself, which brings with it the ability to grow, to seek a new and better and more abundant life.

We want to be sure, when we speak of the gift of self awareness, that we are aware that it is not an end itself.

Viktor Frankl carries this two steps further. He says that even self actualization which is beyond self awareness cannot be the aim of human existence. He says that human existence is essentially self transcendence and that a side effect is self actualization.[16]

At any rate, these are some thoughts on what it means to rise above mechanicalness, to begin to reach out toward the actualization of the human potential. Thinking about it is the first step toward getting out of the rut.

Freedom

Freedom is the most highly treasured of all God's gifts to people. Human freedom is not like the freedom of birds to fly the friendly skies, migrating with the seasons, nesting and soaring into the wide open skies as they choose.

Even paralyzed or imprisoned human beings can be free because freedom is not identified with mere mobility.

From the imprisonment, hunger, dehumanization and torture of a Nazi concentration camp, Viktor Frankl could write of the "last of the human freedoms" — the ability to choose one's attitude in a given set of circumstances.[17]

It seems to me that the first or last or basic human freedom is just that: the freedom to control one's outlook on life, on the meaning of life, on the ultimate destiny of one's life — even when every other freedom is taken away.

Human beings are free when the spirit holds reign over the body, the emotions, the imagination.[18] The freedom of the spirit-controlled person is contrasted with the slavery of a person to the world, the flesh, and the devil. Human beings are free to choose God and the things of God, and they are equally free to choose material things and self gratification. If, in the exercise of this freedom, they choose the things of the spirit, they are still free. If, in their free choice, they choose self indulgence, then they sell their freedom to that.

Having this freedom means each person has the power, the privilege of making his or her own decisions. It means each can march to their own drum.[19] $-6-$

"To become free is to become real live children of God and be part of the universe inhabited by these real live children of God."[20]

The special gift of human beings is freedom of choice. The special gift of Christians is the glorious freedom of the children of God. They are so complementary to each other that I have purposely discussed them together here.

Emil Brunner says there is no slavery comparable to the slavery of masterlessness. For then, one is slave to $-7-$ one's own passions, or to the worst of all tyrants, the ego, or as the Bible expresses it, to sin. . .The sinful one is the one who recognizes no Lord but oneself. One can get free, only by getting free of the tyrant, sin. This liberation can occur only by the acceptance of God as our Lord. And we accept God as our Lord only by being saved through Christ from our sin. [21]

We are free to be awake, to arouse ourselves out of the stupor of our sleep walking, out of the paralysis of lying, imagination, negative emotions, excessive talking. We are free to choose a more abundant life — but few do.

Ability to Make Value Judgments

A gift closely related to freedom is the right and responsibility to choose this rather than that. I can choose this because I have weighed all the angles. I have looked at all sides of it. I can make a value judgment. This special human characteristic makes people moral beings. Animals cannot make value choices. They can appear to do so, but they are following the pull of instinct, appetite or conditioning.

Many times in my life, I find myself, like an automaton, choosing this rather than that by force of habit. For example: On my way home I plan to go several streets past my usual exit from the freeway, but my car "automatically" turns off at the regular place. I am "sleep walking" in my driving. I am not exercising my human potential of being awake, choosing, making this deliberate choice in preference to that.

By the same tokens, animals cannot consciously think of "reasons" or consequences. Human beings can, but all too rarely do.

Along with the right to make value judgments goes the responsibility which is part of being intelligent, free, and able to choose. "Human beings are responsible through their decisions for the consequences of those decisions. This is part of what is meant when we think of ourselves as moral beings.[22]

Dr. Norman Pittenger adds another important consequence which follows from the gift of free moral choice. "Because we are human, possessed of rationality, able to make significant free decisions, and living in a world in which everything is interconnected and interelated, one of the works of our human nature is willingness to accept responsibility for decisions made and their consequences.

"And in no area of experience is this so obvious to a person of integrity as in the realm of sexual experience. . . Irresponsible sexual behavior is not fully human. . .It reduces a person from the status of 'lover in the making' to that of the beasts."[23]

The ability to make value judgments is a distinctly human gift and it is particularly noticeable in the area of sexual decisions.

The Power to Love

This leads us into the next characteristic of authentic humanity, the power to love.

Animals "have sex." Human beings make love. (Making love may include genital activity, but not necessarily. Love and vaseline are not mutually inclusive, or exclusive.)

Without love, human life is seriously incomplete, despite the amount of "sex" one has. Human life requires giving *and* receiving love and friendship. No life is complete without someone to love.

Dr. Pittenger, one of the most loving and loveable persons I know, says that "for us, the defining characteristic is our growth toward becoming genuine lovers in a relationship of caring, concern, self giving and receiving. Toward this we are moving. If not, we are denying our possible humanity and becoming less than fully and truly human."[24]

Denying our possible humanity clearly states exactly what I have been trying to say: rarely do we approach our potential as human persons. Becoming fully and truly human is the thrust of this chapter. Dr. Pittenger has devoted one of his three score books to the subject. It is his excellent book, *Making Sexuality Human.* But the whole meaning of his book, the whole meaning of this book, is lost if we do not wake up to the meaning of what it is to be *human.*

Love is so deeply rooted in what it means to be human that it would be well to dwell even another moment on this subject.

First of all, it is the law of human life as certain as gravity: "To live fully, we must learn to use things and love people,. . .not love things and use people."[25]

Love has to do with the growth of the personality. Human beings grow as persons when their capacity to love expands and develops.

Loving is seen, not as a series of things we do, but as an expression of what we are. It springs from the basic attitude that we have that makes us who we are. It is influenced by what we are trying to become.

Love is the central value and energy of our existence, of our growth as human beings.

Only by being open to the experience of love can we come to appreciate our essential dignity and loveableness as a person.[26]

I've heard people say, "My angora loves me." That may or may not be true. But your angora cannot love you in any way comparable to your ability to love your angora. And if you cannot love your "significant other" with a love beyond which your angora is capable, you are in serious trouble. Your humanity needs some doctoring.

The power to love is a special gift given to make human beings *human.*

Joy is a characteristic that is peculiarly human. Joyless human beings are less than fully human.

Love without joy is pretty sad love. Life without joy is a pretty inhuman life. Someone said long ago and far away and it's still true: a sad saint is no saint at all.[27]

John Powell puts it this way: I am convinced that people are *meant* to live at peace with themselves, filled with deep joy.[28]

Animals can't smile. Human beings are the only creatures blessed with the ability to express unbounded joy. If other creatures can experience joy, it is hampered by the limitation of their ability to communicate it to beings outside themselves. And that's a big part of what joy is all about. Human beings can "make a joyful noise to the Lord" and communicate and share joy with others.

By the same tokens, sex without joy would certainly appear to be a biological function rather than a human function. (Remember the Victorian adage: do it once a year to make a baby with your clothes on.)

The gift of joy is a gift of God specifically given to human beings. Being more joyful is being more human.

Communion with Others

Another human characteristic is the ability to go outside of oneself to communicate with other people, to live in mutuality with other people.

The fully human person, by virtue of being human, and in fulfillment of the fact of human-ness, goes out of the shell of isolation. Meaningful contact with the world outside of self is necessary for genuine human living. It is best expressed in the art of loving.

My friend, Brian McNaught, dramatically ended his address to a Dignity Conference with an affirmation of the need for love: love of self, love of others.

"We are on a journey. We have a dream. We have journeyed into the core of self affirmation and self-love. We have the dream of loving others with the same care, respect, responsibility, and knowledge."[29]

I doubt that outside comic strips animals can dream dreams of vision. But people can dream. They can have vision. People can reach out to others. People can help others. People can be in communion with others. To be fully human, people *have* to be in communion with others. I agree with McNaught, "If we truly love, we will feed the hungry, visit the imprisoned, care for the aged, walk the extra mile with the person who walks alone."[30]

Meaningful communion with others is a special gift given to humanity. Unless I enter into loving, helping, caring communion with others, I am not fully human. I am more human to the extent that I reach out to others, less human to the extent that I sleep in my cacoon.

A fully human person goes out to others (and to God), not by a kind of compulsive obsessive neurosis, but freely and simply because of the nature of free choice.[31]

In this, as in all ordered living, the fully human person (the person who is awake and striving to reach the human potential) will strive to maintain a sensible balance (in accordance with the gift of being *able* to do things that are sensible). The fully human person strives to maintain a balance between inner reflection and exterior activity in communion with others. To be only introverted, turned in completely on self, or only extroverted, paying no attention to reflection, is not to seek the human potential. Gayelord Hauser in his book of sane and sound advice for living longer says: "The well-balanced, mature person is neither extrovert nor introvert, active and passive, a giver and a receiver."[32]

Communion with others is not only a comforting gift that helps us out of our loneliness, but it is necessary, as well, for growth as a human person — and as a Christian.

Michel Quoist, author of the popular book *Prayers*, in another deeply meaningful book, *The Meaning of Success*, sums up the alternatives of communion with others or isolation in self: "People are torn between two opposing attitudes which they can adopt in regard to their life in the world.

The *one* is basically expansive and relational and is called love. It is love which draws us out of ourselves and makes us community builders, all the way from the community of the family to the community of humankind.

The *other* is regressive and isolating and is called egoism. It is egoism which leads us to retreat from life. If you try to go it alone, you will never attain full maturity. And if you wish to be enriched by others, you have to become one with them, which is just another way of saying that you have to love them. The more you love others, the more adult you become."[33]

John Powell describes the human need for going out of self and entering into communion with others as being inherent in human nature. "Human life is a basic relatedness. The 'I' of me is in constant search of the 'thou' of another and the 'we' of a love relationship. The success or failure of this search is the essential success or failure of human life. To be human is to love and to be loved."[34]

The Dutch Catechism spells out the need to be human by living a life together with others. "Our life is lived in common and this is one of the most inescapable elements of our existence. People cannot exist without other people. They could not speak or think or love otherwise. A person would not even survive birth. We need each other. . . Society is a tissue of personal relationships expressed through mutual confidence and love. Life in common is one of the great answers to the quest for meaning and happiness."[35]

Dr. Pittenger says, "People are social beings, related to and mutually dependent upon other human beings. Nobody exists apart from that human belonging. We are all members one of another."[36]

One's essential human-ness is determined by the ability to go out to others. For the Christian this means a recognition that God is a community of persons and God has created people in the image of God, not as isolated individuals, but as persons invited to a communal life with the triune God and with the whole human family. The Christian needs to see oneself as a child of God. And the more fully one is a son or daughter, the more fully one will be a sister or brother to all others of God's children. [37]

ASSOCIATED CHARACTERISTICS

In addition to the special *gifts* God has given human beings to make human beings human, there are some other *characteristics* closely associated with what it means TO BE HUMAN. In order for us to have a clear understanding of what it means TO BE HUMAN in the development of a Christian sexuality, I want to study with you:

>*The unity of the human person
>*Responsibility for determining our own destiny
>*Self love as distinguished from selfishness
>*The human potential for growth
>*The human search for happiness
>*The goal of human life

The Unity of the Human Person

In both the Old Testament and the New Testament, there are clear references to "the soul," and "the spirit," and "the body." Commentators rarely agree on a definition of "soul" and "Spirit." Different translators of the scriptures substitute varying words.

I have an important point to make here and I do not want it to become confused by the choice of words I use. The important point that is essential to an understanding of what it is TO BE HUMAN is that *a human person* is a unified whole person made up of all those elements that make up one's wholeness.

The self, the "I," the whole person is alive. As I mentioned in the introduction, I cannot separate my breathing from my heart beating and my brain functioning. I want to make the same point about the unity of my body, soul, mind, spirit, emotions, intellect, and all the powers associated with the whole person. In a fully human person, none of these functions apart from the whole person.

Too long there has been handed down in Christianity something of a tradition that dubs the body as bad and the spirit as good. To the contrary, a person is a person. Part of being a person is to have spiritual aspects. Part of being a person is to have bodily aspects. The body is not bad. But it is the creator's plan that the spirit be in control.

The person has functions such as thinking, feeling (senses and emotions), movement (talking, walking, writing, etc.), and sex. To understand what it means TO BE HUMAN, keep in mind that whatever a person thinks, says, or does, it must be said to be the function of the whole person.

A fully human person might be defined as one who has brought the spiritual, emotional and physical elements of life into harmony. A human person is a unified whole, not just a body, not just a mind, not just a spirit. The three elements are so related and so influence each other, that no act is fully human without a proper balance of all those elements that go into a whole human being. The functions of body and emotions are not meant to be separated from the spiritual. Indulgence of the body and its feelings alone can lead to a dehumanizing exploitation of self and others to the total detriment of the spirit. On the other hand, a person who withdraws completely from humanity and material things and tries to live in a completely spiritual vacuum is not being true to the unity of his or her nature as given by the Creator.

Each person is spirit and flesh. The spirit is not added to the bodily nature as has sometimes been assumed. The spirituality of human beings is integral to the nature of the human person as a whole, but so also is one's sensuous or fleshly aspect. The two belong together and function together in everything we say and do. . .

Responsibility for Determining Our Own Destiny

All the things we have already said about the fully human person indicates an essential freedom. Freedom requires responsibility. It is the responsibility of the fully human person to be determiner of his or her own destiny.

The very dignity of being human demands that one act according to a knowing and free choice.[38] This choice does not result from blind impulse nor from external pressure. In the fully human person, choices are the result of intellectual and spiritual decisions. Michel Quoist says: "Your geranium or your dog may attain their proper perfection without making any personal contributions. But your dignity consists precisely in the role you must play in the attainment of your perfection. You have to take a hand in your own self realization."[39]

How is this done? If your body makes all the decisions and gives all the orders, and if the whole *you* obeys, the physical can effectively destroy every other dimension of your personality. Think what this means in terms of appetites for food or drink or sex or pleasure of any kind. What it means in terms of laziness. What it means in terms of emotions of fear, anger, hatred, etc.. The answer is that neither the physical nor the emotional is to be treated with contempt. Both are good, created by God. Both are important components of the human person. But the spirit must make the decisions for the body and the emotions. The one who puts the spirit in control acts humanly. The one who puts the spirit in control is determiner of his or her own destiny.

It is all too easy for would-be human beings to be slaves of their own bodies, instincts, emotions. The fully human person is capable of making value judgments and directing one's life according to an ideal. For the Christian, this is the Christian ideal of life in union with God. Only the spirit can direct such a choice. But it is possible because of the gifts human beings have received, because of our ability to know ourselves and the world in which we live. Human beings have been set free from the tyranny of nature, made determiners of our own destiny.

A fully human person is an actor, not a reactor. In a fully human person there is no such thing as surrender to senses or emotions (be a reactor). Emotions are not biological or psychological necessities. When the spirit is in control a fully human person can change his or her emotional patterns (be an actor).

There are many subtle ways in which a person can be cheated out of being determiner of one's own destiny. A woman who chooses a professional career is all too easily put in a position of surrendering her prerogative to be herself by a society which says she ought to be a mother and stay in her home. Young homosexuals are denied the right of self actualization in many ways by a society which subtly traps them into "finding a nice spouse and settling down" or drives them in subtle ways to instability and insecurity by non acceptance or ostracism. The fully human person needs to ask "Who am I?" and reflect upon the answer and become determiner of his or her own destiny.

God doesn't need any human person. God created each human person out of love. If a person rejects God, that person is only half a human being because a whole human being in the design of the Creator is created in the image of God, and is offered a share in the very life of God. The one who would be determiner of his or her own destiny is one who has turned his or her life completely over to God. Without thus getting in harmony with the plan of creation, one is less than what it is possible to become.

Self Love as Distinguished from Selfishness

Egoism is an obstacle to full humanity. The reach of each person, in the language of Chardin, is upward and outward. The person turned in on self is less than human. In one sense everything that is wrong about human life and experience can be summed up in egocentric living. Egoism, selfishness, whatever it is called, is the enemy of fully human living.

A popular saying these days can be a handy cover up for egoism. "Sorry, but this is the way I am. I was this way before I met you. Why should I change?" John Powell says this is a handy type of motto and delusion for a person to have around who doesn't want to grow up.[40]

Once a person comes out of the protective shell of self and recognizes his or her limitations, welcomes others into their life and enters into meaningful communication with them, then the personality will begin to be enriched and life will become more human.

On the other hand, self acceptance is a requirement for fully human living. A joyful acceptance of God's unfailing love is certainly the beginning of an understanding of one's personal value, human dignity, and essential loveableness.

Paul Tillich says: "Self is good, self affirmation is good, self acceptance is good. Selfishness is bad, because it prevents both self affirmation and self acceptance."[41]

Many psychologists and theologians are expressing this basic truth about fully human living. A deep understanding of and a serious effort to achieve true love of self is the beginning of all human growth and happiness. The essential need of human nature is self esteem, self appreciation, self celebration.[42]

Self acceptance and self love is a most important reality of a truly human life. It is the beginning of all other human love. This kind of self acceptance empowers one to live fully and confidently with all that goes on inside of one. Such a person is afraid of nothing that is or could be a part of one's true self. Such a person is liberated to go out of self and seek a meaningful relationship with God and with others. This self acceptance is a deeply felt and joyfully experienced delight in which the *whole* self finds fulfillment in working toward self realization.

The Human Potential for Growth

Being a fully human person implies a dynamic process. I am different today, I have experienced more of life. I have experienced new depths of love. I have suffered and prayed. I have lived some more. I am different. *Being* a person really means *becoming* a person. So we are never fully human. We are on the way to becoming human. If a person functions freely and fully with all the human gifts and powers, that person will be on the way to growth. That is the human destiny, not perfection, but growth.[43]

To be human is to grow. Failure to grow marks one as moving out of the path of genuine human advance. This path is simply a line of growth consistent with the intentions of the Creator. A "proper human person" is one who under-stands what human life is all about and accepts and grasps the responsibility to *do* whatever is within his or her power to advance and to assist others in their efforts to grow.

The preceding paragraph borrows ideas from Dr. Norman Pittenger who describes himself as a process thinker, that is, one who believes that human beings are not static, fixed, unchanging beings, but rather "becoming." This indicates a dynamic movement or direction in which each human being is going forward toward an actualization of their potenti-alities or is failing to move forward to that actualizing. And people do this in commmunity with other people, to whom they are related, by whom they are affected, and upon whom they exert influences.

– 11 –

From the Christian point of view, this means that the created human being, a composite of material, psychological and spiritual "stuff," is given freedom to use this "self" and all its "stuff" to move in the direction which will best bring that being to genuine "personhood," to the greatest fulfill-ment of his or her destiny as a child of God. It is a sad observation that so few of us in the whole human family even approach realization of our full human potential.

The Human Search for Happiness

The searching, restless yearning that every human being experiences is implanted in human nature, like the urge for sexual pleasure, to motivate human beings to move forward, not to wallow in stagnant inactivity, not to languish in lukewarmness, but to seek the unification of all people and the perfection of all things, to work for transforming the world, to help bring all people, including oneself, to the Omega point.

The goal of civilized living is contentment and happiness. It is inherent in the nature of human beings to work to change the world.

For the Christian this means, if the world is going to be Christianized, it has to be humanized. It is the duty of the Christian to work to this end.

For the Christian, Christ, living, sustaining, empowering is at work within each human person who identifies with Him.

For the Christian, Christ gives a whole new dimension to humanity. The dimension of destiny.

The Goal of Human Life

Finally, in the study of what it means to be human, it should be remembered that one needs to be authentically Christian. This places humanity in the only setting it can have for the believer: The movement of all things that started with God toward God as the ultimate destiny.

Human life in God's eternal intention was to be life in Christ. God never had any plans for merely "natural" people. Human beings are created for the purpose of entering into union with Christ. All humanity is meant to be God's family, while still remaining uniquely free. The intention of the Creator was and is that human beings become more fully human as they become more fully alive in Christ.

REVIEW OF CHAPTER 2

To be fully human is to use all the special gifts given to humanity. To be human is to be what God intended us to be when God created us human.

Human beings are different from animals and have a potential seldom achieved.

We can think about the purpose of our existence and choose this course of action, or that, for a reason.

God created human life and said it was good and went on to make men and women in the very image and likeness of God, and gave human beings the choice of completing their humanity by accepting the likeness of God, or not.

Most people fall short of their potential as human beings.

The marks of authentic humanity include keeping the spirit in control, being truly aware of oneself, exercising the freedom to make spirit-controlled choices and value judgments, allowing love to govern one's interpersonal relationships (learning to use things and love people), living joyfully in communion with others.

A proper understanding of human personality sees the whole person as a unity of physical, psychological, and spiritual aspects.

Human beings unlike any other earthly creatures are not pre-determined by their creator. They are free to determine their own destiny. They can choose the freedom of the spirit or the bondage of the flesh.

Self love and self acceptance are necessary for living a fully human life. Selfishness is contrary to living a fully human life.

Human beings are not static, created in a mold, and fixed to live out a predetermined pattern. We can grow and move toward our potential, searching for happiness, becoming more happy and more human as we become more fully alive in Christ.

STUDY QUESTIONS — CHAPTER 2

OPENING EXERCISE

Place yourself somewhere on this "self acceptance" line.

SELF ACCEPTANCE _____ SELF DOUBT
100%   50%   100%

If you feel you have 100% self acceptance, your mark would be at the left end of the line, etc. In turn each person in the group shares with the others where they placed themselves and why.

1. What is the significance of the human ability to ponder the purpose of our existence? Does thinking about where you are going help you on the journey?

2. In what way is the "Parable of the Eagle" helpful to you? What is its significance in the chapter, "To Be Human"?

3. How do you feel about being created in the image and likeness of God? How does this touch you personally? What does it mean to you? Answer: "To me it means that I . . ." How do you feel it is true, meaningful, significant to you?

4. How does "primacy of the spirit" work? How does the spiritual aspect of you exercise control in your life? Share with the group some of your struggles or thoughts about this. (Remember how St. Paul tells about his struggle in Chapter 7 of the Book of Romans?) How does primacy of the spirit affect sexuality?

5. Is it really true that we tend to be very mechanical? Do you agree with Professor Ouspensky that we are prevented from achieving our human potential because we really don't know ourselves and are victims of lying, negative emotions, etc.?

6. Do you usually want to be free? Would you rather some authority gave you rules to live by? What do you observe yourself doing with your freedom?

7. There is no slavery comparable to masterlessness. What images

are brought to mind by this? What does it mean? Is it true? If so, how does it keep us from being fully human?

8. Why is the ability to make value judgments particularly noticeable in the area of sexual decisions? How does this make sexual decisions "more human"?

9. In turn, each person in the group give an example of using things and loving people, or using people and loving things. Discuss how a person becomes more human by loving people and using things.

10. Divide into two groups for five minutes, each group reporting back ten things that characterize either "making love" or "having sex," but not the other. After the report, discuss the difference.

11. Read the paragraph. Discuss growth as a person; growth as a Christian. Relate this to being fully human.

12. As a group, brainstorm a list of cliches, attitudes, or customs that would dub the body as bad and the spirit as good. Discuss the wholeness of a person: body, mind, spirit!

13. Becoming suggests growing. Discuss the difference between being a person and becoming a person, being human and becoming human. Is it discouraging to you to know that you never arrive, that you are always on the way?

CONCLUDE:

Offer each person an opportunity to thank God for one of the special gifts to humanity and ask God for a strengthening in some area of being human where she or he feels a particular need.

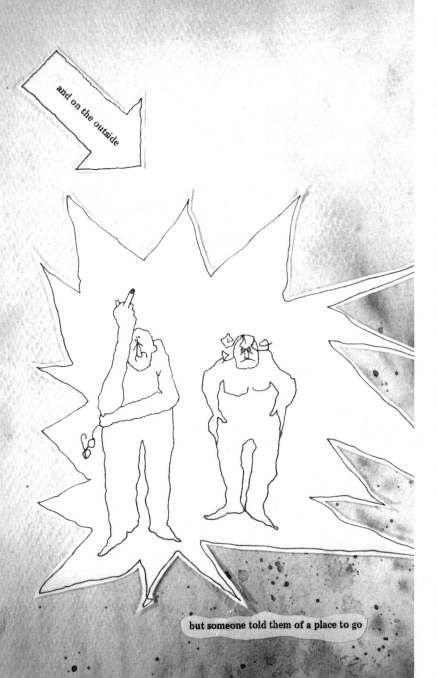

where they were taught about

GOD

3

To Be Sexual

MAKING HUMAN SEXUALITY HUMAN

The preceding chapter, "To be Human," presented a study of what makes a human being *human*. We discussed some of the distinguishing characteristics which raise humanity to a state above the rest of the animal kingdom. To be fully human is to be free, responsible, self loving and self giving, in communion with others, somehow in union with God, spirit-controlled, consciously moving toward a goal, determiner of one's own destiny, intent upon becoming what one can become.

Created Sexual

Now as we enter into a study of what it means "to be sexual," we need to remember all the things we said about what it means "to be human." Being sexual is another dimension of being human. Part of one's physiological, psychological, and sociological make up is being sexual. Sexuality is rooted in the body, but grows out of the whole person.

"The body has a place in God's plan for a redeemed humanity. And this means that sexuality has a place too. . . Sexuality does not determine our lives as persons capable of living in a community — being human does that. Yet sexuality is an essential part of our personal lives. If we fail to take account of it, we are forgetting the kind of person we are. We are as God made us, and that includes our sexuality."[1]

There are a lot of things this chapter is not. It is not a study of biology, nor a study of sex acts, nor a study of the morality of sex acts, as such. It presents some reflections on what makes *human* sexuality *human*.

Human Sexual Behavior

Animals are biologically moved to mate in the sex act in order to comply with the instinct to produce offspring. Human beings feel what must be a similar biological urge. Every person experiences the persistent and demanding urges of sexuality. Craving for sexual satisfaction, for sexual relief, for sexual union permeates our being and frequently dominates our behavior to the exclusion of all else. Our sexual hungers frequently tell us to do things which appall our more rational and spiritual dimensions.[2]

It might be pointed out that human genital sexuality expresses itself in six ways: masturbation, nocturnal orgasm, heterosexual petting, homosexual relations, sexual contact with animals, and heterosexual intercourse. This is Dr. McCary's terminology.[3] It may or may not be objective. I don't agree with his classifications, if they are meant to give an accurate and complete picture. They do point to some of the *types* of possible human sexual expression.

The following is a very short summary of some of McCary's extensive, documented statistics and analysis of human sexual behavior.

Males

Teen age boys have a very strong sex drive and are capable of almost instant erection. Four to eight orgasms a day are not unusual, with only minutes or seconds required for refraction between. Sexual release is desired with little or no emotional attachment to the sex object. If no sexual partner is available, they will normally achieve sexual release through masturbation and nocturnal emission.

As a man approaches his 30's, he remains highly interested in sex, but the urgency is less acute. Erections still occur quickly. But by the late thirties the refractory period between orgasms has lengthened to 30 minutes or more. Slackening continues through the forties.

By 50, the average man is satisfied with two orgasms a week, with a refractory period of 8 to 24 hours.

The truth needs to be known about America's 25 million people over 65. (I'd talk about the people in other countries, but I don't have readily available statistics. I suspect they exhibit some similar tendencies.)

In spite of society's myth that it is "not quite nice" for older people as in "dirty old men" to have sexual yearnings, they do.

The loss of erectile ability is not a natural part of the aging process. A man does not lose the capability of erection because of age. The older man is often able to maintain an erection for a considerably longer time without feeling the ejaculatory urge that plagues younger men.[4]

Kinsey statistics show that men over 65 average at least one orgasm a week. Psychological or sociological causes are more often at the base of sexual "failure" than physiological causes. Since the vast majority of older men do not show physical disability as a deterrent to sexual frequency, the causes must be primarily psychological. Some of the causes described include monotony, career, fatigue, overeating or over drinkin, weakness of the spouse, fear of failure.[5]

Masturbation is found in more than 95% of American men. It continues beyond adolescence in most men. 25% of all married men above the age of 60 also masturbate.

Homosexual relations are far more frequent among males than is generally known by the homophobic public. 37%

(that's more than a third and not so far from half) of *all* men have had homosexual experience to the point of orgasm sometime in their lifetime. The statistic zooms to 58% in single men under the age of 35. These statistics should shade the meaning of the finding that "4% of all white males in the United States are exclusively homosexual all their lives." and "10% of the population is homosexual" as a rule of thumb.

A surprising percentage of men (6%) turn to homosexual relations after they are 60. Why? They stated that they felt a great empathy for their male companions. In fact, they felt that the sexual activity was of less importance than the warmth and sensitivity they found in their partners. The overwhelming need was for affection. "As people grow older, sometimes their need for affection also grows, and the need for sexual satisfaction may increase accordingly."[6]

Females

"Women's sexual awakening is a slower process, not reaching its peak until the late 30's or early 40's. Women do not appear to experience the same sexual urgency during their lives that men do. In their teens and 20's the orgasmic response is slower and less consistent than it is in their 40's. In their 30's. . .women begin to respond more intensely to sexual stimulation. They also initiate the sex act more frequently than they did in the past.

"Women in their 50's and 60's may experience a slight decline in sex drive and are usually less preoccupied with sex than in their earlier years. But they still seek out and respond to sexual situations, and masturbation. . .is quite common.

"Although a woman's sexual resonse moderates as she ages, she remains quite capable of multiple orgasms — even until her late years. She apparently maintains the same physical potential for orgasm at age 80 that she had at age 20."[7]

Masturbation is not uncommon among women. 50% to 80% of all women masturbate sometime in their life. On an average, those women who do masturbate, do so regardless of age or marital status about once every two to four weeks. Women tend to masturbate more after teen age years up to middle age and after that it remains fairly constant.[8]

Homosexuality seems to be somewhat less common among women than men. Most female homosexuals appear to be bisexual, but by no means all. It would seem that about 3% to 9% of all women can be considered predominantly homosexual.[9] The sexual experience of greatest importance and most cherished by the lesbian is embracing and close total body contact.

Finally, I want to mention that sexuality seems to pervade the thinking of human beings. In a survey of 4000 people it was found that "males between the ages of 12 and 17 think about sex once every two minutes. This rate continues into young adulthood and drops to once every five minutes in middle age (40 to 45) and finally tails off to once every ten minutes after 65. Females give thought to sex every two and half minutes in middle age, and once every twenty minutes after 65."[10]

If these statistics are true, or any ways near true, I sincerely believe they provide a very good reason why we should spend some time meditating upon what is "Christian sexuality."

The Hunger for Sex

I think I have shown enough statistics to indicate that sexuality on the level of sex urges and sexual behavior is not restricted to a few "oversexed" human animals. It's pretty popular from "cradle to grave," as they say. And we might as well not entertain any other myth.

Eric Berne says there are six hungers of the human nervous system that are almost as essential for survival as food and vitamins. Among them are stimulation, recognition, contact, desire to penetrate and to be penetrated, plus

—1—

89

structure hunger and incident hunger.[11] Without dwelling on his complicated psychology, we can summarize it all in one: "Most people have a hunger for human contact, at least of sight and sound, and in most cases for touch and stroking. Again we see that such contact may actually make the difference between physical and mental health or breakdown, and even between life and death. Of all the forms of sensation, the one preferred by most human beings is contact with another human skin."[12] "We can call all these hungers," he says, "and sex is the most exciting way to satisfy them all at once."[13]

"Sexual intimacy is a mixture of all nature's elixirs, which has more healing powers than all the mineral waters of Europe, all the trees of the tropics, and all the herbs of China."[14]

Some of the sexual implications of touch are captured in this selection from a Carl Rogers book:

"There is nothing so beautiful and beautifully human as to be held, hugged, loved. To feel the warmth and sincerity of another person. To give, in turn, comfort, strength. Words can often deceive; but an embrace — the truth is conveyed by something other than sound.

"Why are we so afraid to touch? Because to touch means — SEX.

"But don't you see? There is no black or white; but a whole continuum in between. Yes, touching, holding, hugging, carries sex. The most distant, coldly executed handshake is sexual, even in its denial of emotion.

"The way to deal with touching is not to de-sex it, but to acknowledge the existence of sensuousness. Accept it. If I can accept the experience of contact, I will no longer be troubled by it. If I accept the responses it touches off in me, I will probably discover not fear and repulsion, but the true content of the hug — love, warmth, joy."[15]

This is saying, "Yes, touch is sexual."

It is also saying, "But, of course, all that is sexual is not genital."

90

And most of all, it is saying , "Hey, look! Touch, sex, sensuousness, communication of love, warmth, and joy is good, real good."

That brings us, then, to an attempt to define "sex" or "sexuality."

The Meaning of "SEX"

"Sex," "sexual," and "sexuality" are words which are subject to varied interpretations. Each person's rear view mirror of past experience and exposure will dictate how sexuality is interpreted.

My cousin Rodney and I got our earliest understanding of sex from the barnyard on his father's farm in the hills of Ohio. We learned a lot from observation. Nobody ever really explained it to us, but he told me about the wondrous things that were going to happen after the bull went "pee-pee" inside the heifer. We experimented with going "pee-pee" on various plants around the barnyard, but it didn't seem to make little plants spring up.

A person who has been exposed to the neon SEX signs of the Hollywood message parlors and has seen their walking advertisements at the front door has an image of what SEX means, what "SEX: NUDE GIRLS — 24 HOURS" means. And so do the neighborhood children. They understand it about as well as I did in the barnyard.

Those "girls" standing in the doorway or working inside, have their own outlook on what it's all about. A country "girl" in Arkansas may have a terrifying or a beautiful idea of what "sex" is, depending on how her mother interprets it to her.

With Little Help from the Churches

Traditional church teachings have aided in obscuring the true meaning of sex and human sexuality.

After centuries of Roman Catholicism's "Thou shalt not *enjoy* sexual pleasure in marriage" and "prostitution is a necessary dimension of social morality (St. Thomas),"[16] very little progress was made by the reformers. Luther taught that sex in itself was not sinful, but his near contempt for the role of women in this world spoiled the freshness of his outlook on sex. Calvin, like Luther, felt the purpose of marriage (where the man was boss) was for procreation and to restrain the sexual appetite. Sex within marriage was *permissable*, if carefully controlled.[17] "The churches, both Catholic and Protestant, continued to perpetuate the idea that women were inferior, that their role was confined to the home (having babies), that sex was primarily for procreation."[18]

"This was the dominant view of the Christian churches throughout the nineteenth century. The changes in attitude toward sex, marriage, and family which slowly began to take place in the twentieth century were made in spite of and not because of the church."[19]

Dispelling the Shadows of Ignorance

Lack of knowledge about sexuality, what it is, what it does, what it's for, is still prevalent everywhere today. "Guilt feelings aroused by inadequate sex knowledge interfere with happy living, school work, friendships, and marital adjustment. . .Persons who have received an appropriate sex education are less anxious than those without. . ."[20] "It is important to human sexual enjoyment, especially for women, that sex oriented guilt be reduced to a minimum."[21]

The fact of the matter is that the overwhelming majority of people do change their attitudes toward sexuality when they have opportunities for adequate information. Studies show that "about 90% of women and 60% of men report that they eventually came to accept sexual behavior that once made them feel guilty."[22] In my own case, the first big enlightenment was in reference to masturbation. I was a teenager. I had acne. I masturbated. The acne always seemed worse after it happened. My confessor told me it was a "no-no." There was even a rumor that "Self-abuse" could lead to mental illness. I slipped off to consult a "non-Catho-

– 3 –

lic" doctor. "It's quite normal, to be expected, and engaged in by 95-99% of teenagers. No connection with acne." After that I did not masturbate any more than I did before. But I knew that nature was not against me, even if God was. Twenty-some years later I found out that God wasn't against me, either. But I spent twenty-some years of thinking so. And they wonder why I tend toward the neurotic.

To explore some of the dimensions of what makes human sexuality *human*, we can ask ourselves these questions, borrowed from John Powell's, *The Secret of Staying In Love.*

Are you comfortable or uncomfortable with the fact that you are a sexual being?

Are you troubled by sexual feelings and fantasy, or can you accept them as a wholesome, natural, and good part of your human nature?

Do you feel secure as a man or women?

Or do you feel a need to prove yourself?

Does your notion of sexuality pertain to something you do or something you are?

In your own mind and emotions are love and sexuality inseparable.[23] ?

I am not going to attempt to answer these questions. They are for each person to ponder within herself or himself.

Sexuality is, indeed, deeply rooted in the genital, but it is more than genital to the same extent that a human being is more than a body. Human sexuality is more than anatomy and goes beyond the functions of anatomy. Yet, Andrew Greely, the well known priest sociologist from the University of Chicago, tells us: "It is a raw, primordal, basic power over which we have only very limited control."[24] The Dutch Catechism puts the same concept in another way: "It is a marvelous creative force in us. But it is likewise terrifying because of its force."[25]

It Starts with Attraction

The first indication of sexuality in human beings is their attraction to another human being. In convents, novices are taught, or at least they used to be, to keep their eyes modestly cast down, to avoid looking at other persons, especially men. This, of course, was good advice for celibate people. Why? Because it is absolutely natural to recognize within the honesty of oneself an attraction for certain other people. The only way to avoid indulging in this involuntary human trait is to keep one's eyes cast downward.

—4— Both heterosexuals and homosexuals use the word "cruising" for the sexual activity of automatic appraisal of others (even momentarily in fantasy) as potential genital partners. The more or less powerful desire of such indulgence (say at a beach) gets to the roots of human sexuality. In the words of the priest sociologist already quoted, "No matter how sophisticated or how mature or how self-possessed or how casual or how cool we may think our approach to sexuality is, we are all basically 'boys and girls' on the beach" (cruisers).[26] Sometimes, he says, this is more obvious than other times, but it is never, repeat, *never*, totally absent.

Father Greely says this brief and powerful experience of their own sexuality is not only not immoral or perverse, but a revelation of fantastic (and unruly) forces which quite literally can be called godlike.[27] In other words, even the basest human sexual attraction does not need to be as low and biological as purely animal function. Somebody has said that the most libertine of all sexual freedom would be if everybody raped everybody they felt like raping whenever they felt like, wherever they felt like it. That's low. That's base.

On the other hand, the brief, but powerful, electricity which flows from the momentary contemplation of sexual union has been described as an experience of a touch of divine unity.[28] Indeed, there is a wide range of difference between this outlook and St. Augustine's guilt-ridden legacy to the modern world in which he connected all sexuality with the fall of the human race from the favor of God in the Garden of Eden.

Sexual Pleasure

In a moving testimony about her sexuality, Karla Jay says, "For many years I struggled with my sexuality. I agonized, in childish journals and journals not so childish, hoping to discover my real needs, and to separate those from

94

artificial needs that cripple and drain me."[29]

Now, she says, she is still searching, but "I feel it some-times in the arms of my lover. I taste the taste of how it will someday be to love, to be free. . .I want our feet to love as well as our genitals. The tender place behind my knee. Her delicious cheek. I want to roll over and over, like in the fields of childhood. I want to giggle, laugh, sing, grunt, mutter, groan, pant, smile, be suspended in time, go over the water-fall. . .I want to feel our breathing all over my body. I like touching. . .touching her touching myself touching herself touching ourselves touching each other. . ."[30]

What is this sexual thing? "Sexual arousal in humans, both male and female, springs from psychological as well as from physiological sources."[31]

Dr. James McCary, a Christian educator whose popular *Human Sexuality* was distributed by the Book of the Month Club, explains what it means to surrender to sexual pleasure in a human way. "To abandon oneself in an uninhibited expression of love and excitement, to have these manifesta-tions eagerly accepted, to receive in turn spontaneous and equally unrestrained expressions of love and desire: these are the ingredients intrinsic to a sexual relationship in its deepest and fullest measure. People who confine their lovemaking activities merely to the search for orgasmic release soon learn that sex can become quite boring. The degree of pleasure and fulfillment derived from sex is great or small in direct propor-tion to what has been given."[32]

To the Roots of the Personality

When we speak of our sexuality we speak of something that pertains to what we are, not something we do. We are sexual beings. Karla Jay captures something of what this means in the physical and psychological realms in her descrip-tion of masturbation. "Really experimenting with mastur-bation was the big transition for me. . .Not masturbation the antisocial, narcissistic, infantile fixation that Freud dreamed up, but an acknowledgment that sexuality is *inside* each one of us, not a gift or lesson *another* bestows if we only surrender ourselves to it. I define masturbation in the broadest sense as a woman understanding and loving her own body, learning to give sensual and sexual pleasure to herself and exploring her changing rhythms, paces, and needs. All that I learn, I am free to celebrate and share whenever I choose with my lover. Free to begin to break down the rigid categories of what sex is with another and what sex is with yourself."[33]

Sexuality forms the most profound aspect of the human personality. It is sexuality that aids a person in being genuinely human. The Interfaith Statement on Sex Education points out that sexuality is part of the whole person and an aspect of one's dignity as a human being.[34] Sexuality, while rooted in the genitals, permeates the whole human personality.

Thus it can be said in utter truth: sex is primarily something we are, not something we do. It relates to our very being rather than to the functions of our being.

This is important as one reflects on the aspects of sexuality that distinguish it as peculiarly human. It is a *personal* quality rather than a biological function. Being sexual is ingrained in the depths of the personality. It goes to the heart of the wholeness of a person. It is part of being a physical, emotional, spiritual person.

The Quest for Meaning

Human sexual behavior is, more than anything else, a quest for meaning. *Human* sexuality is guided by what is specifically human in nature and by what gives fundamental meaning to human life.[35] That is why Greeley can say it is necessary to view sexuality in the context of the human propensity to seek meaning in behavior.

Animals move by instinct, stimuli, reflexes. Human beings make choices because of their meaning for proximate or ultimate ideals. Specifically, the fully human person can ponder: For me sexual union with this person means such and such. I choose to enter into this union because it has this meaning for me or us." The animal merely reacts to

-7-

96

the opportunity to perform a physical function. The search for meaning in sex is a specifically humanizing aspect of sex.

But, as Dr. Pittenger points out, "to say that human sexuality is for the procreation of children and for propagating the human race is to miss the important meaning of sexuality. It reduces this sexuality to the animal level, to the biological, leaving nothing to the distinctly human."[36]

Human beings are "equipped" sexually with the same kind of organs as are members of the higher animal kingdom. But, often to the disgrace of their humanity, human beings do not use this equipment in a specifically human way. Even so, human beings are not merely talking, laughing, more or less educated gorillas with a comparable sexuality. "Nor can their sexuality be reduced to simple animality. Whatever may be the case of creatures in the animal world, human sexual nature has its specific human characteristics and these make it different from, even though it is related to, animal sexuality."[37]

Sexism

The whole problem of our sexist, patriarchal, male oriented culture can be traced to a total misunderstanding of what it means to be sexual. "Western culture and religion associates man with rational logos and heavenly being, and woman with sensuality, passion and earthly being."[38]

"In modern times this has led us to think of man as naturally assertive, analytic, and manipulative; and women as interrelated, contextual, wholistic, and we have enculturated men and women to fit this masculine-feminine model.

"In addition, those characteristics and roles associated with men in Western society have been highly rewarded and given prestige, power, and honor; while those associated with women have been regarded as not worthy of economic reward or social prestige."[39]

Dr. Letty Russel, a professor of theology and women's studies at Yale University Divinity School, makes a most profound contribution to the understanding of human liberation and "sex role" and thus to sexuality in her theology of human liberation, *Human Liberation in a Feminist Perspective: A Theology.*[40] Its deep implications and theological perspectives go far beyond the scope of this book and it is recommended for those who want to get into the deeper waters of the trends of theology today.

Because a woman is *human* in all the ways we have described in the preceding chapter, "To be Human," more and more women are coming to perceive that their biology no longer necessarily defines their destiny.[41] Women are not legs, bosoms, vaginas, or wombs. In line with these realizations, men and women have become increasingly aware "that new lifestyles are needed in the areas of family and marriage. . .Women and men are beginning to explore alternatives such as communal marriages, serial mating, single parent arrangements, cluster families, polygamy, homosexual arrangements. In the Hebrew-Christian traditions, and in various societies, the shape of the family and marriage roles have undergone many different changes over the centuries. To assert that only one arrangement, such as the nuclear family, is possible, is simply to deny the historical and social facts."[42]

Dr. Russell goes on to quote Dr. Harvey Cox that in the history of *Biblical* religion we have had patriarchy, concubinage, celibacy, group marriage, and serial monogamy. We should not invest monogamy with the sacred significance of being the only legitimate Christian or human form of familial structure.[43]

Dr. Russell concludes, "New forms of human sexuality might provide a basis for new life styles and roles for women and men, when the experimentation is done, not in response to commercialized eroticism, but out of deep regard for the partner as a person. . ."[44]

And More Sexism

If all the above seems to apply primarily to heterosexual people, gay people could well examine their own patterns of role playing and sexist behavior. Although more or less liberated from some of the obvious male-female (and usually male-dominated) sex roles, gay people find themselves falling victim to more subtle forms of sexism and role playing.

Gay men do not ordinarily "use" women in sexual relationships. But both gay men and gay women could examine their language, their thought patterns, and their expectations of the people they relate to. It is my observation that certain things are said and done in the gay community that tend to perpetuate patterns of heterosexual role playing and sexism. — 10—

We observe such expressions as: "Come on, girl"; "Hurry up, Mary"; "My woman. . ."; "I'm the butch one. . ." (usually a non-verbal communication); "I don't do that. Of course, I don't go that way. . ." Along with these we find expressions that betry agism: "With the boys. . ."; "With the girls. . ."; "The gay kids. . ."

The point I am trying to make is that the validity of the homosexual mode of love expression is not enhanced by aping traditional male-female interaction (especially in its oppressive manifestations.)

There is nothing wrong with male-female relations (with whomever on top in the kitchen or in the bedroom, if there needs to be somebody on top). But in male-male, female-female relations (as in female-male relations) there should be a spontaneity and naturalness that the partners are comfortable with, rather than a depersonalizing attempt to live up to some preconceived concept of what or who is "butch" or "fem." — 11—

And Some Syndromes

Jack Nichols offers some advice to men and I think it applies to women, as well. "If a man has been taught to neglect feeling,. . .if he catagorizes sex as a function of the genitals,. . .if he is programmed to achieve,. . . he has divided his sexual life into technological time categories and is in a rush to consumate his affection."[45]

In his excellent chapter on "Sexuality," Nichols makes some interesting observations about two syndromes often associated with men. I would label them "performance syndrome" and "penetration syndrome."

Speaking to heterosexual men about "performance," Nichols says, "Men must be freed from 1-2-3 thinking about what they are supposed to be able to do when they relate to women sexually. . .Masculist values provide many of the agressive, success-oriented, sex-conqueror fantasies that fill thousands of so-called erotic books crowding today's market. . ."[46]

In reference to what I call the penetration syndrome," Nichols writes, "The values impinging upon sex today are obvious in the words used to describe it. . .The words imply that someone, presumably a woman, is being restrained or pinned, either above or below, and hence the word is tinged with a degree of hostility."[47]

It seems to me that human sexuality is not really human if it is forced into preconceived "rules of performance" rather than experienced with all the freedom that marks truly human living.

A Liberating Sexuality

Harvey Cox, well known author and professor at Harvard Divinity School, observes that "there are still large elements of compulsion in the sexual life of modern human beings which militate against maturity, freedom, and fulfillment in community."[48] He goes on to say that the Christian gospel calls people into freedom and away from the bondage of any kind of depersonalizing legalism. It insists that human beings in order to be full human beings must choose their own mode of sexual experience and participation.

This participation, in the context of the reflections of this book, needs to be in line with what makes a human being *human*. This seems to be what Dr. Cox is saying, too. Human sexuality is uniquely liberated, for the most part, from the control of instinct, but surely not from the rovings of imagination. Human beings are the only beings in creation with real sexual freedom and therefore with moral responsibility for the use of their sexuality.

Because of the gifts of humanity, human beings are able not only to question their identity, but to know their destiny and to know how to use all their faculties and gifts in their quest for self fulfillment.

Good: Created by God

In the Genesis story, the doctrine is found that human beings were fashioned in the image of God. John Wynn, author and educator at Colgate Divinity School, says this means that our understanding of our sexuality is hidden in God in whom we live and move and have our being.[49] Paul Lehmann, professor of theology at Union Theological Seminary, says: "Our present concern is to follow the long Biblical journey from the image of God to the image of Christ, from creation to redemption, and try to suggest how the search for sexual meaning may find in that journey a perspective and power through which freedom may be joined with responsibility in sexual experience and behavior."[50]

Thus, as it is true of humanity, so it is of human sexuality: it has been created by God, consecrated from the very beginning. What God creates is good. Nothing is profane: no thing, no person, no part of the anatomy, no aspect of human life.

Among the relationships essential for the full development of humanity, and therefore for the development of sexuality in the design of the creator, is a relationship with God. It is the unique dignity of human persons that they *can* enter into a relationship with God, knowing that they are created out of love, knowing that they are loved as they are.

The Longing for Belonging

The yearning to get out of oneself, the eternal desire to be, rid of loneliness, the ever present hope for unity with another has human dimensions unknown in other species. The *way* of human life is to be interdependent.

The *way* of sexuality is to relate to one another. The Presbyterian scholar, Robert Bonthius, goes on to explain: Human beings are made for relationships. Their sexuality is a dramatic form of that relatedness. Human beings are made for interdependence. Sexuality is a pervasive form of that interdependence.[51] Sexuality is the somatic (bodily) expression of our belonging to the universe, of our belonging to one another, a power which prevents us from living in isolation, which reflects itself in our dependence on another.[52]

There must be some way of converting Barth's quotable quote into non-sexist language. "To be man is to be fellowman." "To be human is to be in communion." That's not as catchy, but it says what Barth said in the language of another age. Woman isn't woman alone. Nor is man, man alone. In fact, it is not good for man or woman to be alone. To be fully human, an individual must not be an individual.

Communication, language, the ability to transmit significant messages is a gift given in a special transcendence to the human family. Language is expressed in symbols: words, acts, signs. The sexual act is seen as a sign that two people on the search for the identity of each, have found the identity of each by moving through bodily union beyond their separateness toward the fulfillment of each in the other.[53] Animals seek completion of the biological function. Human beings seek union, identity, interdependence.

Neither Promiscuity nor Prudery

Certainly in this description of human sexuality there is no reason for anyone to perceive an endorsement of promiscuity, nor, on the other hand a call to prudery. This chapter is trying not to enter the area of what acts are good or bad, what specific behavior one should choose. It is reflecting on characteristics which will be the marks of truly human sex.

One of these marks will be maturity and the ability to make "grown up" decisions. Nobody is responsible for what they do in their sleep. But grown ups are responsible for staying awake. A two year old is not humanly responsible for what it does with a loaded hand gun. That is why it is so painful to see a child beaten or humiliated for touching or playing with his or her "privates." Truly human sex means that a person is able to be responsible.

St. Paul often refers to his recurring theme of freedom. In Christ, the believer is free from sin, death, and the Old Law. In Galatians 5:13 the Apostle tells the converts: *"You were called, you know, to be free, but be careful lest this freedom becomes an excuse for letting your physical desires rule you. Instead, let love make you serve one another."*

In the exercise of human freedom (which is freedom to be human, to decide, to search for meaning, to seek communion with others, to work toward an ideal) men and women are not endowed with a sex instinct innately directing their sexual behavior toward clearly defined goals. Nor do sex acts performed by human beings automatically become expressions of love. Human sexuality merely endows the individual with the potential capacity of becoming sexually mature (human, that it), and relating to a partner in a loving, uniquely fulfilling, mutually responsible way.[54]

Love: The Norm for What is Human

Freedom and responsibility then lead to love as the ultimate norm for what is human in sexuality. Human sexuality, Dr. Pittenger says, as a physiological and psychological reality, is the basis for the human capacity to love. It provides the possibility for the person as a total organic being to exist in a relationship of love. Human sexuality is an expression of human loving. "This means that its concrete expression in genital activity and associated behavior *must be related to love* in the most intimate fashion (in order to be human). Love is the reference. Love is the criterion. Love is the basic significance of human sex."[55]

What is Love?

Dean Ferm says: "The focus for proper sexual behavior is love. There is no word in any language more difficult to define than love."[56]

It can be used to mean *lust*. The dictionary defines lust as an intense sexual desire. That doesn't explain it. One author gives it the connotation of self aggrandizement. This means the building up of oneself, adding to one's power or position, almost forcefully taking things for one's own needs.

It can be used to mean *philia*. This is friendship, brotherly or sisterly love. In the older days thousands of high school students could tell you all about it after studying Cicero's *De Amicitia* in the original Latin.

It could mean *eros*. Sometimes this is called the drive to create. Webster says it is love directed toward self-realization. Another describes it as the urge toward higher states of being and relationships.

It could mean *agape*. Webster define this simply as "love." I believe this is the fourth of Webster's nine definitions of love (with many additional sub-divisions). "Unselfish, loyal and benevolent concern for the good of another." It is the selfless love exemplified in God's love for God's people, in Jesus Christ's self-sacrificing death on the cross. It is The Love which has its primary concern for the other.

In this book we are aiming primarily to show the connection between human sexuality and *agape* love. The connection: successful sexual relations are caring relations in which each partner is sensitive to the needs and desires of the other. This "caring" then continues well beyond the experiences of sexual arousal and release.

Affection

When sexuality expresses a genuine love between two persons, there will be a need for expressions of affection and tenderness. Affection is expressed in exterior ways by signs, by touching, by kissing, by mutual responsiveness in body union.

Dr. McCary explains that "many people in our culture, especially men, have difficulty entering into a warm, close, loving interchange with others. Little boys are often taught that to be tender and compassionate is to show characteristics of being a 'sissy.' Little girls are admonished that it is 'forward' to be warmly responsive.

"Growing up in an environment that restricts positive emotional responses makes it likely that the individual

104

will learn to express only negative emotions, such as anger and hostility.

"Nonetheless, these people grow into adulthood with the abstract knowledge that some warm emotional exchanges are vital and expected in successful sexual interaction. But because they learned in their formative years to express only negative emotional responses, such people will actually instigate quarrels or fights with their sexual partner in order to express the only type of emotionality they understand. Persons who have never learned how to express tenderness, or who are afraid to do so, will often ignore the person with whom they are sexually involved, or make belittling remarks. They want to demonstrate their commitment but, not knowing how to use the appropriate positive emotions, they use the only emotional expressions that they are familiar with — the negative ones."[5][7]

Dr. McCary goes on to explain a related hindrance to the uninhibited expression of affection in loving sexuality. A sexual partner will often accuse the other of showing affection toward them only when they are "having sex" on their mind. The accused will deny this. What happens is that the one commences simply to show affection to the other with no ulterior motive in mind; but in the process of expressing affection, especially if the other responds warmly, the initiator becomes sexually excited. The other then judges only in terms of the final outcome. What happens then is usually neither loving, nor sexual, nor joyful. Negative emotions again take over.

Fortunately people can learn to allow themselves the joy of experiencing close, warm, loving relationship. When they learn that free expression of affection is nothing to fear, that it is not a barometer of effeminacy, (Is there something wrong with effeminacy?) all their human relationships, including the sexual one, will be fuller and happier.

I have dwelt on this matter of expressing of affection to call back to mind what we said in the introduction. We are all too often machines, reactors, not in command of our behavior. We let out past and our habits, our rear view mirror govern us. If we want to live a *human* sexuality, in warm and happy sexual relationships, then we must be especially *awake* to the factors that militate against this realization of our beautiful potential.

Hangups

There happens to be an unbelievable number of possible hangups that can cheapen or destroy a beautiful sexual union. I am going to list a few more of these. First, to show some extremes, I am going to list some of the reasons given by 1000 wives for their refusal to have sexual relations with their husbands:[58]

1. Fear of pain in the initial intercourse
2. Opinion that the sex act is nasty or wicked
3. Impotent husband
4. Fear of pregnancy
5. (Imagined) small size of vagina
6. The couple's ignorance regarding the exact location of the wife's sex organs.
7. Preference for a female partner
8. Extreme dislike of the penis
9. Fear of damaging husband's penis
10. Fear of semen

We could go on to make quite a lengthy list of complaints in love-making. Let's apply the following to any lover relationship.

*Partner just wants to "have sex"
*Partner just wants to "make love"
*Partner is too selfish
*Partner is always in a hurry
*Partner is not sufficiently concerned about satisfying the other sexually
*Partner is not gentle in approach
*Partner is too crude, forceful, unromantic
*Partner is too romantic
*Partner is too unimaginative
*Partner is too mechanical and ritualistic
*Partner is too inhibited
*Partner won't let go and really enjoy orgasm
*Wants partner to anticipate sexual needs

*One partner feels no need to ver-
balize sexual needs; the other
should know
*The other guesses wrong
*Partner condemns the other, ver-
bally or silently
*Partner rewards the other's correct
guess only with silence

If I have listed enough hangups here to make us conscious
of the games we can play in love making, I will have accom-
plished my purpose. For further information, Eric Berne,
author of *Games People Play*, has a chapter titled "Sexual
Games" in his book, *Sex in Human Loving.*[59]

A Happy Acceptance of Sexuality

When the sexual drive is truly human, it is a healthy
and wholesome force which leads to a deeper actualization
of the whole human capacity for life. This calls for a happy
acceptance of one's sexuality. It will be something to be
thankful for. It is a gift of God. "If sex relations are what
they ought to be for Christians, they will be nothing less
than celebration.[60]

Paul Lehmann says the presence and power of Christ
means that sexuality and humanity (and one might add
Christianity) belong together. Joy and peace in belonging are
the fruit of joy and peace in believing.[61]

Truly human sexuality should bring a happy acceptance
of one's sexuality. Human beings are sexual beings. This is a
good thing, nothing to be afraid of, nothing to run away
from. When it is recognized, accepted, and "rightly" used,
sexuality is both ennobling and splendid, somehow an earthly
sign of the creative principle of love itself, the God who is
cosmic love, or Cosmic Lover, as Dr. Pittenger puts it.

To accept oneself in all one's sexuality is a way of accepting oneself as a social being created to live in mutual
helpfulness and affirmation with others. The way a man or

woman handles sexuality is a pretty good indication of how they handle the rest of their life, according to Bonthius.[62]

A happy acceptance of one's sexuality begins with an understanding of what it means to be human and sexual (and Christian). It includes an understanding of the problems and possibilities of sexuality, its hungers and its satisfactions. Sexuality is part of the human condition. And that's something to be thankful for. But self acceptance, as was pointed out in Chapter II, is a requirement for a fully human life. A joyful acceptance of one's sexuality in the light of the unfailing love of the One who bestowed this gift is certainly a step toward that abundant life that God became flesh that we might have. Again, a cause for rejoicing. It's something I like to think about. God became human, sharing in the humanity and sexuality given to humanity, in order that the people of creation would not only be able to have a more abundant life, but that it should be a redeemed life, a share in the divine life itself. That does not make humanity with its sexuality an end in itself. It makes it just what it should be in the order of things, another means to self realization in the upward and outward evolution toward total unity with God.

In summary, to be sexual in a human sort of way means that the human-ness of the person is inundated with sexuality, but sexuality becomes human only when it seeks meaning, is guided by love and pursues its pleasures with responsibility.

REVIEW OF CHAPTER 3

Being sexual is another dimension of being human.

Sex urges, sexual thinking, and sexual behavior are persistent and nearly universal in human beings.

Sexuality is deeply rooted in the genital, but it is more than genital. It is a marvelous creative force and difficult to control. It springs from psychological as well as physiological sources.

Being sexual pertains to something we are, not something we do. It is a personal quality, rather than a biological function.

More than anything else, *human* sexual behavior is a quest for meaning.

Sexism has its roots in faulty understandings of sexuality. As male over female chauvenism is lessening in some segments of society, certain patterns of heterosexual role playing are perpetuated in the gay community.

In eliminating roles from sexual behavior, there should be a spontaneity and naturalness that the partners are comfortable with, without being victims of a performance syndrome or a penetration syndrome.

STUDY QUESTIONS – CHAPTER 3

OPENING EXERCISE

(Allow each person in the group to answer the six questions without comment from the others.) What is your answer to each of the six questions? – ● –

1. Are these statistics helpful to your understanding of human sexual behavior? How? Or, do they turn you off? Why?

2. "Preferred by most human beings is contact with another human skin . . . There is nothing so beautifully human as to be held, hugged, loved." Are these your feelings? Tell how you feel about these sensations. Do you feel they make you human in a good sort of way?

3. "The fact of the matter . . . a high percentage of people eventually come to accept sexual behavior that once made them feel guilty. Can you point to any such experience in your own growth toward sexual maturity? Do you feel you are better or worse for it?

4.. Do you agree that every person experiences, at least secretly in the inner self, an attraction for certain other persons, which is translated into "cruising," secret or open, if entertained to any extent? Is this attraction an evil inclination? How should a person feel about this type of impulse?

5. As Karla Jay describes her sexuality and her masturbation, do you have a feeling of wholesome, clean, God-given sexuality? Or something else? Like what? Can you feel yourself in her place? Do you feel good about the feeling you get as you picture yourself in her place?

6. When you think of your sexuality, do you think of sex as something you do or something you are? Is this a new idea for you? Do you feel sexuality is part of your whole personality or just genital activity?

7. Is the statement, "For me . . . for us" too idealistic to be useful? What relation does it have to "tea room" sex? How do bars and baths fit into this? In what way can you give meaning to sex so that you feel more like a fulfilled human being?

8. Do you feel that somehow your sexuality is different from that of gorillas or other animals you may have observed first hand? How?

109

9. How is sexism related to sexuality? How might oppressive sex roles be described as a perversion of *human* sexuality?

10. Is the author too hard on homosexuals? Is he stereotyping by charging that some gay people indulge in subtle forms of sexism?

11. Describe spontaneity and naturalness as contrasted with preconceived concepts of what or who is "butch" or "fem"?

12. How does a "penetration syndrome" fall short of the ideal for *human* sexuality?

13. Does Dr. Pittenger's statement mean there is to be no sex unless there is love? Does this mean that the bars, baths, one night stands, sex on the first date, tea room sex — are all out? Are they all in the same category all the time?

14. What is human sexuality? How is it related to "agape" love?

CONCLUDE

Offer each person in the group an opportunity to share a short "sentence prayer" thanking God for some aspect of his or her sexuality and forgiveness for some abuse of human sexuality or petition for something in connection with his or her sexuality?

who had a son who was also .... different

DIFFERENT ...

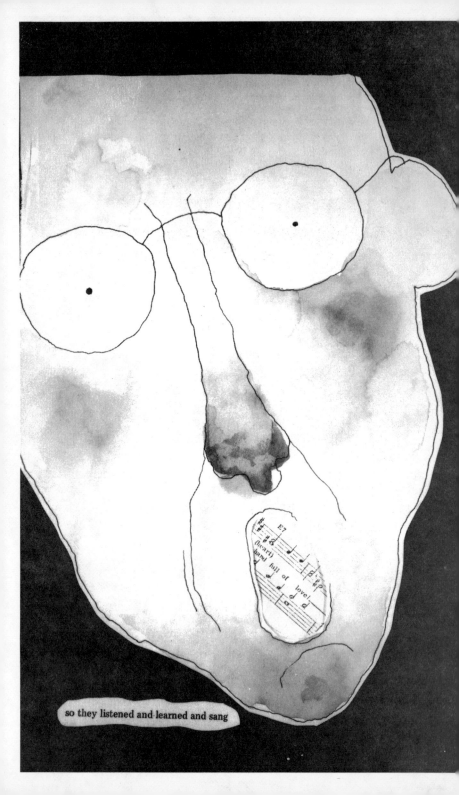

4

To Be Christian

LIVING IN CHRIST

What does it mean to be Christian?

Who has a right to the name?

In a sense all the preceding reflections have been a study of what it means to be Christian. In the Christian perspective, to be human, to be sexual in a fully human way, is to be Christian. In this chapter the focus of the reflection is turned to the totality of immersion in Christ, which is a way of making humanity and sexuality Christian.

There is no way that one can consider what it means to be Christian without relating everything to Jesus Christ — the meaning of his birth as a human being, the meaning of his life and message, the meaning of his death, and the meaning of his resurrection.

The Incarnation

The uniqueness of the incarnation has a special meaning for this study of Christian sexuality. There can be no getting around the fact that sexuality is quite deeply rooted in the flesh. And the fact that Jesus is God in the flesh says something very significant about sexuality. In a very revealing way it carries the "God saw that it was good" of Genesis to the specific context of human life as lived, enjoyed, suffered, and fully experienced by God in person.

Jesus "in the flesh" is God "in the flesh" and this raises flesh to a dignity that should make all human beings shout for joy: "Wow! The creator has joined creation. That calls for a celebration!"

And that celebration is what this chapter is looking into. The marvels, the wonder, yes, the mystery of God entering into the bloodstream of bodily, physical, human existence is food for thought for a lifetime, far beyond the scope of this chapter.

To be Christian means to be in Christ. Just as the incarnation means that God enters into flesh, so "to be Christian" means that a human being enters into Christ.

Accepting Christ

All the classic Christian concepts of repentance, conversion, regeneration are well known and necessary. But it's more important for me to turn from sin and live in union with God in Christ than it is for me to be able to define "metanoia."

All too often we identify a Christian as one who believes a body of theological truths. "I have attended the instruction classes. I am ready to become a member of the church. Of course, I am a Christian."

That "of course" means, "Well, you can take that for granted. I wouldn't think of joining any other religion, especially since I've come this far in my studies of what the Christian church teaches."

Usually anyone who takes it for granted, and would have you take it for granted, "Of course, I am a Christian," has managed to cover up something by that "of course."

Have you ever heard a person gasp when somebody (perhaps impolitely) asks, "and when did you become a Christian?" For evangelical Christians the year and the place is not enough. For them, the exact day and moment of the most important moment of their life is indelibly impressed on their consciousness. I remember seeing on television a rejuvenated eighty-four year old preacher testify that he had preached the gospel for sixty years before he "became a Christian." Now that should be enough to cause you and me to reflect a moment or two on the "when" of it for ourselves, since "of course, we are Christians." Of course!

Many people feel being a Christian is a very personal thing. It is. For me it goes something like this.

"God loves you and has a wonderful plan for your life." Yes, that's the first spiritual law taught by the Campus Crusade for Christ and many other evangelical groups. Yes, I believe God loves me. See, I'm a believer.

People are sinful and separated from God. (The second spiritual law). Yes, I recognize my sinfulness. I even denounce my separation from God. I repent.

People are constantly trying to pull themselves up by their own bootstraps, trying to reach God through their own efforts. Pagans and people of every civilization have tried to do this. People want to make contact with God, but their own efforts always fall short.

Jesus Christ is God's only answer to the sinfulness of people. Through Him, people can know and experience God's love and God's plan for their life. (The third spiritual law) Yes, I know Jesus is the answer. See, I'm a believer. See, I really am a Christian.

To know that Jesus Christ is God's answer to people's sinfulness is not enough. To believe that Jesus Christ is God is not enough. To be that kind of believer is not enough to make one a Christian.

The fourth spiritual law is dramatized in the scriptural scene: "*Behold I stand at the door and knock: if anyone hears my voice, and opens the door, I will come in.*" The essential step in letting Christ in is to open the door.

To become a Christian it is not enough to know that Christ is God, that Jesus is Lord. To be *His*, you need to make him *yours*. To be a Christian, you need to open the door to Him for you. He does all the rest. But you need to accept Christ as your personal Savior. So it's not: yes, He is; but, it's: yes, He is for me.

115

The fourth spiritual law is that we must receive Jesus Christ as Savior and Lord by personal invitation.

Now there are all kinds of things that can be said about that in various types of theological language. The fact remains that this kind of acceptance implies an identification with Jesus. Just as He identified with humanity by actually becoming a man, so human beings actually identify with Him by entering into a mutual relationship with Him.

Identification with Christ

When we accept Christ as our personal Lord, and therefore accept an identity with Him, we make a commitment to Him. It's not simply a matter of *saying*, "Jesus is Lord of my life." If I am going to bring all my humanity to this commitment — and I must — then this acceptance means that I accept a certain mentality, a certain world view.

A commitment to Christ is not simply a matter of trying to imitate what Christ was like in the gospel descriptions. If I would be a Christian, it's a matter of bringing my thinking and my point of view more and more in union with the way in which Jesus sees life here and now.

That is what identification with Christ means. That is what the incarnation means *for me*. That is what it means for me to be a Christian.

More than anything else, to be a Christian is to live a commitment to Christ and His way. "*I am the way, the truth, and the life.*" "*Without me, you can do nothing.*" "*I am come that you may have life and have it more abundantly.*" "*I am the resurrection and the life.*" "*My peace I leave with you.*" And with St. Paul we can say, "*I can do all things in Him who strengthens me.*" These are promises of what "His way" can do to raise humanity to a new level.

This is why accepting Christ is called being born again. This is exemplified when a person chooses to be baptized by immersion, goes down into the water, dies, buries the old self, the sins, the separateness, the rebellion, and then comes up out of the water, washed, cleansed, renewed, reborn, alive in Christ, accepting the salvation and the freedom offered by

116

this new identification with Christ.

In accepting identity with Christ, "*It is no longer I who live, but Christ who lives in me.*" I accept an identity as a child of God, being identified with the Son of God. Then I need to face who I am. I am this person who is a child of God. This new birth has done something radical to me. The special gifts of humanity were already amazing gifts. Now I must face the reality that I am offered a share in divinity. In some theologies this is called grace. In common language, it means, as a saved, redeemed, purchased person, I am walking with God. God lives in me. Because of Jesus, I am able to accept a level of being which unites me with God.

The love of God experienced through the gifts of creation, and through the complete and total self-giving of Jesus to the last drop of His blood, shows us the height, the depth, the breadth of God's love for us. And then God calls us: "Children of God." What a value this places on our humanity. The unbelievable love of God for me, in spite of my weakness, my sinfulness, my separateness, my rebellion..

Too long have I resisted. Can I point to the day and the hour when I fell on my knees and cried, "Yes, Lord, I accept your love? I accept your salvation. Take away my sins and make me one with you. I want to live and move and have my being in you. From now on you are my Lord. Thank you for your love. I give you my love in return. Thank you, Jesus."

The thing about becoming a Christian is not that it takes away our weaknesses, or even our sinfulness, but that it gives us the assurance of salvation, the peace of forgiveness, and the ecstasy of knowing we are loved in spite of our weaknesses, and yes, in spite of our rebellion against God.

This new identity as a Christian calls us to bring our own personal consciousness, our awareness, our understanding, our love, our choice, our sexuality, the whole of our humanity into this new creation.

Primary Commitment

Now it's important to take a look at the *commitment* involved in saying, "I accept Jesus as my Lord. I am a Christian."

Let's take a look at a very weak comparison. There was a man who made a decision to live on the Equator. He knew it was going to be hot and humid there. He made the decision, the primary commitment, if you will, to go there, knowing what he was getting into. Once that decision was made and he went to live at the Equator, it would be inconsistent for him to complain about the climate, to wish he were some place else, to dress for winter weather, to act, speak, or think in any way inconsistent with his primary commitment.

A person is free to go to the ballet, or stay at home. But after making the primary commitment, one needs to face all the other factors (lesser commitments): the cost of the ticket, perhaps the cost of a companion's ticket, the gasoline cost, the parking cost, the program cost, the dinner or coffee cost, perhaps the tuxedo rental cost, cancelling other appointments, and whatever.

Once primary commitments are made, secondary commitments need to be made that make sense in line with the primary decision.

If I make a decision for Christ, that is, if I make a commitment to Christ, I am taking a radical step. I am making a primary commitment of major proportions. And I should be ready to have it influence *all* my secondary decisions.

Another example of commitment is seen in the athlete. The athlete makes the decision to seek perfection in the sport of choice. Then other decisions must serve that decision: willingness to work, willingness to put that first above other pleasures.

My son, John, a football player of some accomplishment, made a decision early in his high school days to excel in shot put on the track team. As a freshman, he made the varsity team because he could throw farther than any other person in the school. He continued to excel in his sophomore year. In his junior year he won several awards including first place in his league. At the end of his junior year, I received a letter from him: "I've been holding my weight to about 210 all year. It's going down and I'm firming up and getting stronger. Next year is the big year track-wise. That's why I'm practicing all summer. I'm going to be state champ. That will take a lot of work, but I plan on doing it." It took a lot of work. He placed in the top five in the state competition. But, he did it because the primary commitment was important to him. There must have been times when almost anything would have been more fun than throwing, throwing that heavy ball, trying to better his own record. But the primary commitment was excellence. Smaller decisions had to fall

into line with that.

Commitment is contagious. Now his next younger brother, Rick, is following in his footsteps, winning his share of awards in his first year of track competition.

Now in some ways, commitment to Jesus is a lot easier than commitment that calls for hard work. Commitment to Jesus is a commitment to *be* in Jesus, to think, to speak, to choose, to act in communion with Jesus, that is, in union with Jesus. It's not really even a commitment to work hard. We can't "work our way into heaven." If we surrender our lives and our wills completely to Jesus, we probably will want to work hard at a lot of things *because* of that commitment, but not *in-order* to earn any reward.

So, the comparison with the athlete (or the artist, or the business person who works hard to reach a goal) is not focused on reaching the goal, but on the fact that a *primary* commitment is made and all other decisions must be made in such a way that they make sense under the first commitment.

So, if you say, "Jesus is Lord," and you are willing to make this a real commitment, rather than a hollow statement, then you get into deep territory. When you make this commitment, "*You are to love the Lord, your God, with your whole heart, your whole soul, your whole mind.*" This is a scriptural way of saying you are to love God with the whole *you*, your physical part, your psychological part, and your spiritual self.

"With all your mind," means that God expects people to think through all the implications of their commitment. Jesus was more knowledgeable of human nature than a good many people give him credit for being. When Jesus said this, it was another way of saying that the human being, in order to be fully human, needs to bring all parts of the human oneness into a balance in whatever decisions are made.

Results of Commitment

If this commitment to Christ is real, it will be reflected in some noticeable results.

Making the primary decision to be in Christ means entering into a very special partnership. Are you a Chris-

120

tian? A "yes" answer means something very specific. Not "Yeah, I guess so." If someone asks you if you are a spouse, it means something very specific. Who is your spouse? If you say you don't have one, you are not a spouse. It's the same way with being a Christian. Unless it's a partnership with Christ, it's nothing.

Being a Christian, then, calls for a new loyalty, which goes beyond all other loyalties. "For me, to live is Christ." It is a complete and total surrender. Faith is a surrender. Paul Tillich says somewhere that faith does not mean the belief in things hard to understand. Faith means being grasped by a power that changes us. Surrender to this power is faith.

Falling back into the arms of Jesus, as it were, in this type of responsible surrender, one hears a voice, "Give me your life, and I will give you life with God forever. I will give you freedom and together we shall overcome."

With this as our primary commitment, we find we are faced with some important questions. "What am I really for? What do I want most? What is my deepest concern?" If we know the answers, our primary commitment, whatever it is, should evoke a lot of enthusiasm.

If one has a real commitment to Jesus, one not only has a real loyalty to him, but a whole lot of enthusiasm towards being "in Christ," for working with Christ to establish justice, to cure disease, to abolish hatred, to build community, to do everything so that God's will is done on earth, as well as in heaven. Then one begins to make all decisions in accordance with the basic decision.

Unfortunately it doesn't very often happen that a person lives the human potential to the full. Most people find themselves falling short both at the human level and at the supernatural level. The more real one's commitment is, the more realistic one's life will be, the more consistent all decisions will be. There will no longer be a dichotomy between one's life as a Christian and one's life in the world.

A friend of mine, Arnie, called. He was reflecting on some of the things that impressed him about Malcom Boyd's *Are You Running With Me, Jesus?*[1] He was especially impressed by Boyd's prayer in a gay bar. Arnie feels God is wherever Arnie happens to be at the moment. "I feel God is with me just as much when I (a plumber) am unclogging somebody's toilet, as he is when I am in church. And," he continued, "God's with us right now, right here over the phone, where two of us are together in His name." When people feel that kind of union with God, their life becomes peaceful. They have a Christian attitude about things.

Another Boyd prayer captures what Arnie means and all of us feel so often. "Lord, you're over there where I'm keeping you, outside my real life. How can I go on being such a lousy hypocrite? Come over here where I don't want you to come. Let me quit playing this blasphemous game of religion with you. Jesus help me to let you to be yourself in my life — so that I can be myself."[2]

Michel Quoist sums up this total immersion in Christ in more elegant language. "The person who sincerely wants to live the Christian life is not content to restrict this life to certain defined limits, to certain clearly religious acts, to the mere minimum which satisfies the letter of the law. Authentic Christians want their faith to develop maturely. They want their faith to give meaning to every aspect of human existence. In short, they want to bring a new point of view to their life, to their relationships, to their whole world.[3] And that new point of view is the mind of Christ. It is the orientation of one's whole person, with all its energies, toward the person of Christ.

God is a lover who wants our whole being, not selfishly or tyranically, but because this is the only way to human fulfillment and God's glory. To accept or reject this relationship is a serious matter.

A genuine commitment to Christ will show in loving relationships with the people in one's life. Love will be the basis for all decisions. Reconciliation, justification, forgiveness, regeneration bring human beings to a new freedom where everything is decided from the position of love, the love demonstrated on the cross of Calvary.

Witnessing

A result of Christian commitment (turning one's life and one's will over to Jesus) will be participation with Jesus Christ in His mission of bringing all people to know Jesus

Christ and take part in His work. If that sounds something like a circle, it is. But it's supposed to be an endless series of self multiplying circles. A study of Christ's mission reveals Christ bringing love into human lives. The action of the priesthood of all the people, then, is essentially entering with Jesus in to His work of unifying all people under the impact of love. Sharing one's relationship with God with other people must be a noticeable result of really making a commitment to Christ. Unless a person is enthusiastic about witnessing for Christ, it can seriously be questioned whether one is enthusiastic for Christ.

Praying

Along with witness, prayer will be a regular part of one's life. Entering into this relationship (Jesus-Thou) requires communication. If Jesus really is Lord of one's life, there will be an inner need for the communication of adoration, praise, thanksgiving, repentance, and petition.

Fellowshipping

Identification with Jesus Christ requires identification with His church. Some may want to draw the line there. "Wait a minute! I accept Jesus as my personal savior, but I want no part of the hypocrisy, bureaucracy, "money-ocracy" of the church." Somebody has said that it is often the case that people who think they are rejecting the church are really rejecting caricatures of it. Thus they are rejecting what they should reject.

There is a rather good rule of thumb for evaluating a church. If you want to know if a particular church (congregation) is the Body of Christ, check it against this simple check list:

> Is it a *worshipping* fellowship?
> Is it a *witnessing* fellowship?
> Is it a *working* (serving) fellowship?

—3—

In this ball game, it's one strike and you're out. If any one of these elements is missing, it is not really the Church of Jesus Christ. Look for a church that meets the test.

123

The church needs to be a group of people, a community, centered on Jesus Christ, worshipping, witnessing, and serving as a community. (And that calls for a book all its own.) Suffice it to say here, that to be a Christian is to identify with Christ and with the Body of Christ. Involvement in the church will be a noticeable result of making the primary commitment to Christ. It follows as a requirement of the decision to accept Christ.

Christian Sexuality

Finally, it will be noticeable that Jesus is Lord of one's whole humanity, the body, the mind, the spirit. As was pointed out above, human sexuality is not something one does. It is something one is. But the same thing is said of "Christian-ness." It is a state of being. I am this person who is Christian because of my identification with Jesus Christ. My sexuality is inherent (inborn) in my personality. Therefore, my human sexuality is part of my Christian personality. If the whole of my life as a Christian is oriented toward the Lord of my life, then I will *live* my sexuality in the mind of Christ.

-4-

-5-

-6-

Being a Christian Homosexual

"How can you reconcile *being* a Christian and *being* a homosexual?"

Because of the frequency of this question, the folowing brief reflection is offered on the subject. Statements on this subject, sensible, meaningful ones, are being offered frequently these days from many sources: The Metropolitan Community Churches, Dignity, Integrity, the gay caucuses of the various denominations, Catholic theologians, an Episcopal diocesan study (Detroit), The Salvatorian Task Force on Homosexuality, statements by general assemblies of some denominations, some of the church press sometimes, enlightened authors such as Norman Pittenger and Patricia Nell Warren,[4] and others.

In this book, the answer really has already been given. In the context in which this book has been written, what pertains to being human, to being sexual, to being Christian, applies equally to being a Christian homosexual. That sounds like a good starting point, but it is only because somewhere wires got crossed, circuits got shorted out, fuses were blown, and darkness entered in — that it needs to be said at all.

If the Old Testament seemed to teach that male-female union was the norm for human sex, certainly, when Jesus freed humanity from sin, death, *and* the Old Law, and gave a new norm, the Law of Love, this norm extended also to the sexuality of the human person. The new principle for the rightness or wrongness of anything, including sexuality, is love.

At the risk of introducing ethics before reaching the chapter devoted to that subject, it would be well to reflect here for a moment on Dr. Pittenger's statement in *Love and Control In Sexuality*. "Sexual behavior is in its proper order when love is central to it and to all modes of sexual expression. License is doing what one wants when and as one wants, regardless of consequences for oneself and others. This is not freedom. It is bondage to the impulses and instinctive responses of the moment. This is likely to produce a kind of existence which is dissipated, scattered in all directions, with no integrity and no point of reference. Human beings are to act like human beings and are to be helped to become fully human."[5]

A result of true commitment to Jesus Christ as a primary commitment will be to live in love — and thus to submit one's sexual expression to the test of love. According to this test, unsatisfactory sexual behavior is that which is selfish, cruel, impersonal, irresponsible, or inordinate. —8—

The same test, the same norm, applies to the heterosexual mode of expression and the homosexual mode of expression (and the bisexual, for that matter). In the context of the preceding reflections on "being human," "being sexual," and "being Christian," the essential goodness of human sexuality makes the first test: Is it human? And then: Is it Christian? The common elements in "both" of these tests is: Is it loving? Does it meet the Christian standard for all human relational behavior?

Alternatives

Can a person be gay and be Christian? Some will say: Certainly it's no sin to be a homosexual as long as you don't practice it. Every Catholic and Protestant theologian who offers a liberal Christian understanding of homosexuality refuses to put God in that predicament.

More and more responsible scholars are rejecting sexual abstinence as a solution for homosexuals. They are offering opinions to this effect: homosexuals have the same right to friendship, association, and community as heterosexuals. Like heterosexuals, they are also bound to strive for the same ideals in their relationships, for creativity and integration. They, too, are required to examine and evaluate their behavior in terms indicative of wholesome human sexuality. . .

The traditional attitude of the churches toward the homosexual has constructed the popular myth that a homosexual cannot be a Christian. This attitude has been characterized by condemnation, hostility, antipathy, demoralization, and total rejection. These attitudes are completely at odds with the approach which is the very essence of Christianity: that all human beings are called to be Children of God.

New Christian movements have arisen because of the traditional attitude of the churches. Gay caucuses have sprung up in some denominations, some with official sanction, some with official disdain. BUT, the subject is no longer being ignored. Just as the immoral aspects of the Viet Nam war finally settled into the consciences of the majority of American people, so also the issue of the injustice of the ostracism and rejection of homosexuals is slowly starting to rise above the zero level in the consciousness level of America.

and pretty soon these people grew beautiful again
on the outside

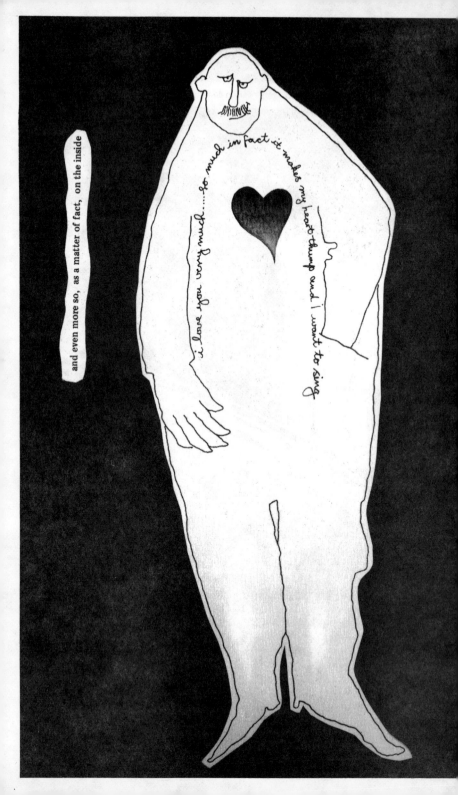

In 1968 the Metropolitan Community Church was founded in Los Angeles by the Rev. Troy D. Perry. It preached God's love for all people and opened its doors to all people. Within a few years it had several hundred members in Los Angeles and had spread through its Fellowship to more than one hundred cities across the nation and around the world. Integrity has begun as a movement of gay persons within the Episcopal Church. Dignity chapters for gay Catholics have been formed in many cities to provide Catholic fellowship and Mass and the Sacraments for gay Catholics, otherwise left to the official teachings of the church or the wisdom of the individual confessor.

In the Roman Catholic Church a study of homosexuality is being conducted under the auspices of the Catholic Theological Society's committee on sexuality. The committee is headed by the Rev. Anthony Kosnik, advisor to Cardinal Dearden of Detroit, Dean of the Roman Catholic Seminary at Orchard Lake, Michigan, and my own professor of moral theology. Kosnik, a scholar of no small repute, reports that the committee of scholars analyzed each biblical reference to homosexuality and prepared their position. Publication date of the paper is fall 1976.

Dignity's Answer

By far the most helpful treatise published to date, in my opinion, is a booklet published by the Dignity National Office, *Homosexual Catholics, A Primer for Discussion*.[6]

This is a no-words-wasted book which intelligently and convincingly answers a multitude of questions about being Christian and homosexual. Although it is addressed to Catholics, I see no reason why it cannot be applied to all Christians.

Speaking of counseling homosexuals, the book says some counselors hold the position that "active homosexual relationships can be counseled not merely as a 'lesser of two evils,' but as a positive good, and as part of God's plan for creation that can be lived out (like heterosexuality) in a positive, mature, and Christian manner which need not necessarily exclude the Catholic gay person from full participation in the life of the church including reception of Holy Communion.

"Generally the priest will want to encourage the person to seek some kind of spiritual counseling to help him/her move into a gay life style that is in conformity with Christian values, and to help him/her avoid sins against love (exploitation, promiscuity, love without responsibility, unfaithfulness) which are found in heterosexual society as well. What the (counselor) is most concerned about. . .is the *quality* of the relationship, and the failures to live up to the demands of a mature, Christian, selfless kind of loving rather than just the fact of genital expression, or the fact that the particular relationship happens to be between two individuals of the same sex."[7]

Whittling Away at the Myths

Most denominations are facing either honest debate, internal dissension, or floor battles at their General Conferences on issues pertaining to homosexuality. The United Methodist Church for example, retained its ban on ordination of self-avowed homosexual persons when the issue was voted on at its General Conference in April 1976.

Father Gregory Baum, one of the most famous of all Vatican II theologians, wrote a surprisingly understanding article in *Commonweal*. "We have ample witness of Christians whose lives as homosexuals are based on mutual love. We must conclude that persons who are constitutionally homosexual *must* accept this orientation and live accordingly. Homosexual love, then, is not contrary to human nature, defined in terms of the mutuality towards which human beings are summoned. As equal members of the believing community, homosexuals are to express their sexuality in a manner consonant with Christ's teaching of love."[8]

In due time, perhaps, the churches will come to public positions where black and white, gay and straight, men and women, will be equally recognized as God's children. The American Psychiatric Association and the American Psychological Association have paved the way in the mental health

– 9 –

field by removing the official stigma of mental illness from the state of homosexuality. In the area of law, the State of California, joining more than a dozen other states, has lifted the stigma of felony from private consenting adult homosexual expression. (A Coalition of Concerned *Christians* unsuccessfully expended thousands of dollars and untold work hours in a tremendous outpouring of energy to get this "ungodly" law reversed.)

Can a person be a homosexual and a Christian? The following comment of Barbara Gittings in *The Same Sex* gives a solid basis for a sane answer: "Homosexuality is not a sickness, nor an impairment, nor a failure, not an arrested development, not a flaw, not an incompleteness, not a distortion, not a sin or a sinful condition. It is not something to be resigned to or endured. The majority of homosexuals would not change if they could. Most important, they should not change even if they could. And this calls for acceptance of homosexuality on a par with heterosexuality and acceptance of homosexuals as children of God on a par with heterosexuals."[10]

The preceding digression has been necessitated by the myths surrounding homosexuality and Christianity. Any effectiveness any effort might have to bring homosexuals to see themselves as God sees them, not as some several thousand years of cultural distortion have caused them to see themselves, will be an asset to growth in the spirit.

Bill

I think I can best express what I think goes on inside the minds of many gay Christians who really love the Lord by sharing the story of Bill. — 10 —

Bill was already middle aged when I talked with him. He was well educated and had been very "religious" all his life. By that I mean, to the extent of his background, training, and personal growth, he had always tried to express his praise, worship, thanksgiving, repentence, and petitions to the Lord as an integral part of his life. For him, religion was never something you put on at times, like a "Sunday suit."

Bill tried to maintain a balance in his Christian life. He set aside sometime each day explicitly for prayer and meditation, communing with the Lord. Beyond this, he was conscious of the presence of God all through the day. Even when he was not on his knees in prayer at home or some other place, he was somehow "praying ceaselessly" as the Apostle Paul admonishes us in I Thessalonians 5:17. Bill was a very active, hardworking person and did not go around with his eyes cast downward. He was involved in many things in the world of people and things that he belonged to. But, by and large, he maintained a recollection of the presence of God. Hardly a minute passed by that he did not momentarily, fleetingly, speak to the Lord. "Yes, Lord," "Thank you, Lord." "God, help me." "Yes, Lord, I know this is your will."

He spent a minimum amount of time each day in scripture reading and other Christian growth reading. He was convinced that a Christian life that does not grow through nourishment withers and dies and gives way to whatever else it is that occupies a persons attention. He found a small group of Christians who had similar ideals of spiritual growth and communion together in Christ. He met, prayed, and studied the scriptures and Christian living "informally" with them.

He knew that his enthusiasm was hollow if it did not involve a commitment to share with others what meant so much to him, his life in union with God, his Christianity. Whenever it was appropriate, without forcing himself on others, from a vantage point of true friendship, he shared with others how important God was to him. He recognized that the best position for him to introduce his friend Christ to a person was from the position of friendship. He was, therefore, a very friendly person and made it a point to become a friend to people that God put in his life. It was only natural that, in God's own time, he would introduce these people to his friend Christ. In doing so he made it a practice to *talk to God about a person before talking to a person about God.*

I really think his Christian life was a beautiful example of a balanced life of prayer, study and action. His action of witnessing to the Lord was solidly based on his prayer and study, on his love for God and for people.

But way down deep in his heart he knew he was a homosexual. Over the years he had sought counsel from both ministers and priests. Some were most loving, even understanding. But none of them was able to help him integrate his homosexuality with the otherwise exemplary balanced Christian life that he was living.

"I simply had to figure it out for myself," he told me. "I prayed and prayed. I studied the scriptures. I even looked at all those Bible passages people quote to point out that God is against homosexuals.

"Then I contrasted these passages with the New Testament pictures of Jesus. *'Love God; love your neighbor.'* He loved everybody, especially those who were rejected or oppressed in His society. He accepted people as human beings. He related to Samaritans (foreigners), women (who were considered inferior), lepers (who were social outcasts), sinners (who were supposedly rejected by God). I realized that I must find that same Christ through the parts of me rejected and oppressed by society.

"What it all boiled down to was that I rejected the God who is a Big Policeman In The Sky and accepted as my Lord and Savior the Jesus of the gospels who proved to me God's love for me.

"Further, I said to myself, Jesus Christ was God in the flesh. God thought enough of human flesh that God entered into it and proved that it was good. I decided that for me the rule of what was good was going to be the facts of Jesus' life and teachings and not the culture of His day or the interpretations of later moralists.

"Then I started to think some things through. I don't know if Jesus ever masturbated, or not. I do know that He gave a tremendous dignity to human life by becoming human. I do know that a very important part of my human life, and His, is sexuality. I also was not naive enough to be unaware of the Kinsey statistics on the near universal phenomenon of masturbation in (95% plus of) all human males and very high percentage of human females.

"Well, I just plain decided that I was going to worship a God of love and understanding, a God who was consistent and logical, a God who does not play games. The God I wanted to worship created human sexuality and said it was good. The God I wanted to worship was represented in the humanity of Jesus. The God I accepted as my God does not seem to have the hangups about wholesome sexuality that "religionists" would have us believe.

"When I was assured by respected mental health authorities that my occasional enjoyment of my sexuality in masturbation was not pathological, I was convinced that God was not going to cast me into outer darkness. In other words, a day came when I was convinced that masturbation was not a sin for me. I didn't do it out of rebellion against God. I did it in accordance with the sexuality given to me by God. It did not separate me from God (sin). It could rather indeed, be part of my union with God.

"Once I was over that hurdle, I began to apply the same thinking to my specific sexuality, homosexuality. I agreed with St. Paul that lust and creature *worship* could separate me from God. I agreed with Jesus that all things are to be based on *love of God and love of neighbor*.

"So, in figuring it all out for myself, I decided that for me the important thing was my starting point. My starting point would be the kind of God I had discovered, not the isolated passages from Genesis, Leviticus or Romans I. Once I decided what kind of God I would worship, I found it fulfilling to worship that God in spirit and in truth, knowing that I loved that God with all my heart, with all my strength, and all my mind. I knew that in worshipping that God and giving that God thanks for all my God-given gifts, I could be absolutely certain of that God's love for me, not because of anything I could say or do, but simply because that is the kind of God I have. I knew then that it was precisely in the rejected and oppressed part of my humanity that I could be

134

most assured of God's love for me."

In talking with this man, in counseling with him, in observing his balanced Christian life, in observing his relationships with other people, in observing the deep mutual love between him and his lover, I had to conclude: *There can be such a person as a Christian homosexual.* Here's one, at least, to prove it.

As a matter of fact I've met a goodly number of Christian homosexuals, not a few of whom were more notable for their Christian-ness than for their homosexual-ness. And that is not to play down their sexual nature, but play up, that is, to emphasize their Christian commitment.

It is no longer I who live, But Christ who lives in me

This chapter, then, has reflected on what it means to be Christian. Acceptance of Christ as Lord means surrendering one's selfishness completely so that, as a new person, the Christian can say, "*It is no longer I who live, but Christ who lives in me.*" This kind of immersion in Christ is a total orientation of one's full humanity, of one's whole being, in this new direction. This fundamental orientation influences all the thinking, talking, doing of the Christian. It means one needs to love God with the whole heart, whole soul, whole mind, with a loyalty that springs from a singleness of purpose. This loyalty will show in enthusiasm for everything that Christ stands for. It will show results in love, in particiaption in the work of the church, in identification with Christ in the worshipping, witnessing, serving community of God's new people. And finally it will show in the way one expresses sexuality according to Christ's Rule of Love.

REVIEW OF CHAPTER 4

To be Christian means to accept identity with Christ.
The fact that Jesus was God in the flesh raises flesh to a great

dignity. Just as Jesus entered into flesh in the incarnation, human beings enter into Christ by becoming Christian.

The way to enter into Christ is to accept Christ as one's personal Lord and Savior by inviting Christ to take charge of one's life. Then, "it is no longer I who live, but Christ who lives in me."

If I accept Christ, I make a primary commitment of major proportions. I take a very serious step that should influence all my secondary decisions.

If I say, "Jesus is Lord of my life," then I must be prepared to love God with my whole heart, my whole soul, my whole mind — with all that is me.

The result of this primary commitment is a loyalty that means "for me, to live is Christ." And this loyalty will be converted into enthusiasm for working with Christ to establish and promote God's will in all things. In short, the result is that my whole person, all my energies, all my relationships, everything I say and do, is turned toward God.

Such a commitment shows in witnessing. Unless a person is enthusiastic about witnessing for Christ, it can seriously be questioned whether one is enthusiastic for Christ.

Such a commitment shows in prayer — communication with God.

Such a commitment to Christ shows in identification with the Body of Christ, a group of people centered on Jesus Christ, worshipping, witnessing, working together. Membership in the church follows as a requirement of the decision to accept Christ.

If the whole of my life is oriented toward the Lord of my life, then I will live my sexuality in the mind of Christ.

The principle of the rightness or wrongness of sexuality is love. Sexual behavior is in its proper order when love is central to it. Unsatisfactory sexual behavior is selfish, cruel, impersonal, irresponsible, or inordinate.

Homosexuals have the same right to sexual expression as heterosexuals and the same obligation to live their sexuality according to the Law of Love. Then their sexuality, too, can be and will be Christian sexuality.

STUDY QUESTIONS – CHAPTER 4

OPENING EXERCISE

It is suggested that the leader invite each person in the discussion group to share his or her answer to the following question in turn without comment from the others (in order to give each person an opportunity to express himself or herself). If there is a desire to discuss the question further, do so after each has answered.

What is the strongest argument you can think of to uphold the position that a person can be a Christian and a homosexual at the same time?

(Or, the following alternate exercise may be chosen.)

Share with the group your testimony of when you became a Christian. (This could also be shared by two's.)

Discussion questions:

1. If the incarnation means that God became a real human person in Jesus, does it follow that Jesus experienced sexual feelings? Did He struggle with sexual temptation?

2. Do you know anyone who has made a "primary commitment" in the author's terms to being a Christian? How important is this for a would-be Christian? What is the basis for your answer?

3. Do you feel your church meets the requirements for being a church: a worshipping, witnessing, working fellowship?

4. What does a primary commitment to being a Christian have to do with Christian sexuality? Do you think this is too "heavy" for some?

5. What does it mean for you to "accept Christ"? Does this have any bearing on your sexuality? Why or why not?

6. Does your primary commitment to Christ affect your secondary commitment to your sexuality? How? (Note: a person has an unlimited number of secondary commitments.)

7. Is it difficult for you to make a "primary commitment" to Christ? Share with the group some places where this is difficult for you.

8. Read the statement. Remember that inordinate means out of control, beyond all good order. Comment on this statement. Would you accept it for yourself?

9. What do you think of Father Baum's position? Agree? Disagree? Shocking? Helpful? Interesting because?

10. Read the story of Bill together — perhaps taking turns paragraph by paragraph. Have you ever met a Christian like Bill? Do you think he is an authentic Christian? Why? What do you think is the most Christian thing about him? Do you have any problems with the kind of Christian Bill is?

CONCLUDE:

Give each person in the group an opportunity to share in the group a sentence prayer of thanksgiving for something they are thankful for in being a Christian.

and it seemed like in just a wink of the eye

Society threw away that Great Hammer

and started sprouting its own kind of beauty

5

To Be Moral

FORMING CHRISTIAN MORAL JUDGMENTS

This book would be incomplete without some moral guidelines. But the disagreements and varieties of approaches among experts (theologians with doctoral degrees and other recognized "authorities") make a person who is not an expert feel like "a fool rushing in where angels fear to tread."

THE HERITAGE

A Hodge-podge

In this chapter I am addressing a situation which is chaotic and badly in need of being put in order. I am attempting to present a systematic approach to deciding what is moral and immoral, for me, in each individual decision that I am faced with. I think such a systematic presentation is necessary because, as historian G. Rattray Taylor observes, "our system of sexual morality is muddled and arbitrary. In fact, it is not in any consistent ethical sense a morality at all. It is essentially a hodge-podge of attitudes derived from the past, upon which is erected a shaky and inconsistent system of law and social prohibition. Some of these fragments from

–1–

141

the past date from before the introduction of Christianity. Some are magical in origin. Others are based on faulty science, prejudices of dominant groups, or taboos to relieve unconscious, irrational anxieties.[1]

If everything that has been said before in this book is properly understood, there really isn't much more to say. One who wants to be moral, in the perspective of this book, will be fully human (with the full powers and uses of sexuality) and radically Christian (that is Christian to the roots). That statement covers a very wide expanse of life. It should cover all day to day situations, the moment by moment decisions.

But still we ask: "How can I know what is right or wrong, good or bad, for me, in this single act, in this free choice I have right here, right now?"

Rule Books

It would be so easy to solve the problem, answer the question, by consulting a rule book. "Now, what was that question? Oh yes: How long can two unmarried people kiss without committing sin? Let's see. They have added a new category for the new morality. Do you believe in pre-marital sex? And there's another one, too. Are the two people of the same sex or opposite sexes?"

'And so if you consult the right paragraphs of the right sections of the right book, you can find out when it's right or wrong, when it's good or bad, when it's sin, and how long you can do it before it is sin.

You've never heard of this book? We've been conditioned all of our lives to look for the catalog of sins. There is hardly a preacher who does not recite the list of "sins" one after the other.

There were such books in history. From the eighth century, the church began to develop a series of penitential books to help confessors give the "right" penance for each sin. These books covered the subject of sex in all its details. Every misdeed was described and elaborated at length and penalties were described for each. For example, the involuntary nocturnal emission was a sin which got a penance of singing thirty-seven psalms. There were twenty-five paragraphs against the "sin" of greatest concern: masturbation.[2]

Sin

In contrast with the whole idea of sins being actual acts, there is another way of understanding morality. Responsible contemporary Christian thought, Catholic and Protestant, does not regard sin so much as specific acts, or as breaking a set of divine commandments. The essence of sin is considered to be the breaking of a right relationship between a person and God.[3]

Some people may be shocked by the viewpoint that sin is not an act or that sins are not commodities to be listed. But consider: Is it a sin to kill? Yes, killing is a sin. What if a one-year-old child accidentally pulls a trigger and kills someone? The act of killing is committed. *There is no sin* because responsibility for the killing cannot be ascribed to the one-year-old child. In other words, the relationship between that child and God was not destroyed or broken.

That is easy to see, but it will be the difficult task of this chapter to present some guidelines for making choices in what is right and wrong in everyday decisions by using a method different from a catalog of sins. Dr. Pittenger says, "some of the views of the new thinkers may scandalize Christians brought up to believe that there is always a plain, straightforward, unchanging, and hence absolute set of moral requirements. The truth is that the new attitude finds its validity in the gospel sayings about love, in the total impact of the figure of Jesus, in the Pauline Epistles, in the main thrust of the Christian moral tradition. '[4]

Change in "Absolutes"

These are some rather pointed examples of things which have changed. The Christian church has closed its eyes for centuries to things that God could hardly have in the book of good acts.

When we look at the history of the Christian church and study how it has fluctuated on many issues, we cannot still affirm that the law of the church is the law of God and what's law is law and that's the end of it.

When we look at things around us, we can find ample reason to suspect that things are not always absolutely right or absolutely wrong. Fletcher convincingly shows that all "rules" except one, either proximately or ultimately, fail to pass all the tests to give them *absolute* validity. The only one that qualifies, always, is the Law of Love.

When we look at the history of the Christian church with a critical eye, or with the help of a Taylor or a Bailey, we can see "situation ethics" applied slowly over the centuries without the advantage of the wisdom of Fletcher's love ethic.

What am I talking about? The situation in the first century, for example, made the church position on slavery come out one way. Different situations in later centuries made the position come out differently. Moralists of a later century can surely point to the Great Crusades and other "holy wars" as not being so "holy". Certain things that were done *in the name of religion* and thus presumably in the name of morality and goodness, in another age, are a source of horror to some Christians today. The Crusades, were condoned, participated in, promoted and supported by supposedly good people. The burning of witches and the torching of "faggots" were holy deeds in the eyes of some.

A more or less chauvenist attitude toward women persists to this day in many otherwise Christian circles. Churches still are not unanimous in their moral judgments on racism, poverty, war.

The once absolute "what God hath joined together" attitude toward divorce has fallen from the list of absolutes.

Today there is little agreement, even among Protestants, on the *pros* and *cons* of birth control (somebody quipped about the prophylactics and contraceptives of the whole matter). The "war" over abortion is another example.

And finally the absolutely impregnable moral absolute is: homosexuality is a sin.

Not only the church has indulged in situation ethics without the advantage of the Law of Love. Harry Truman,

President of the United States, played a massive game of situation ethics before making the decision to drop the atomic bomb on Japanese cities. He had "experts" counseling on all sides. Christian situation ethics would have put love above all the other considerations. If love had been the primary consideration, would the bomb have been dropped?

There have been a lot of inconsistencies in Christian tradition. Not everything that was regarded as good could get a majority vote today. Not everything that was regarded as bad is in everybody's catalog of sins today. Let me make it clear. I am not suggesting morality by majority vote. I am pointing to disagreement and change on things once thought to be "absolutes."

To be sure, evil and hurtful actions exist in our lives. But guilt is another matter. Guilt and sin have to do with our relationship with God and with other people. There is sin, plenty of it. But it is not automatically equivalent to evil. Nor to the breaking of "laws."

Ancient codes, commandments, rules, customs have no absolute significance. (According to Webster, absolute means fixed, irrevocable). They provide us with guidelines. "Neither scripture, nor the church, nor theologians have the complete answer about what is sin and grace." And this is the statement of a Franciscan Friar in a usually conservative Franciscan publication.[5]

CONSCIENCE

So today's Christians find confusion and contradiction. They want to do what is right. They see some irrelevance in lists of sins. They even see some irrelevance in churches and church spokespeople who preach as if there were catalogs of sins. In the long run, and in the short run, they are going to do what they decide is right. There is no such thing as consensus morality, but there is such a thing as free moral choice by free and responsible Christian human beings, who feel that the freedom to choose is better than slavery to legal codes or moral commandments.

Such people are going to form their own conscience and they would like some help, some guidelines for doing so.

Paul Tillich made the observation that perhaps the word conscience should be excluded from all discussions of ethics since its connotations are so manifold and contradictory that the term cannot be saved for a useful definition. But, he decides, this suggestion should not be followed. The word conscience can and should point to a definite reality: the subjective self interpretation of personal life.[6]

Even St. Paul seemed to take over this Stoic concept of conscience and baptize it in the light of his Old Testament learning and Christian insight. For him, it is substantially one's personal judgment of moral good and evil. He refers to this idea of conscience eighteen times in the New Testament writing ascribed to him.

The word itself comes from the Latin "consciens," knowing together; what a person knows within the self and with all that has shaped that knowing.

The Webster dictionary succeeds in stating with clarity what theologians have managed to muddle. "Conscience is a sense of consciousness (knowing) of the moral goodness or blameworthiness of one's own conduct, intentions, or character. Hence, a faculty, or principle conceived to decide as to the moral quality of one's own thoughts or acts, enjoining what is good."

It's important in this post-Pinnochio age to have at least a couple of understandings about what conscience is not. It is not a little voice whispering in the ear. It is not even really the voice of God. It is not a "feeling" of guilt when we do something wrong. It is not intuition. It is not inspiration, not even the guidance of the Holy Spirit or a guardian angel. Nor is it a Jiminy Cricket or the "internalized value system of the culture and society." It is not, strictly speaking, the reasoning faculty of a person making moral judgments or value choices.

It is the whole human person making a moral judgment. It's a choice based on many factors, not merely a result reached by force of logic.

I agree with Joseph Fletcher and situation ethics that conscience is a function of the human person, not a faculty. It is not some kind of control box located just to the left of the pituitary gland. "There *is* no conscience. 'Conscience' is merely a word for our attempts to make decisions creatively, constructively, fittingly."[7]

It is important to note that what we are talking about is something that we do *before* we act. Conscience is a decision before acting, not a sense of guilt after sinning. It can, however, review the rightness of wrongness of an act already finished.

It's okay if people want to have their own definitions of conscience, but to meet the objectives of this chapter, the idea of St. Paul and as expressed in the Webster definition will be put into a formula that has helped many people decide what is right. This formula will be explained in line with the preceding reflections of what it means to be human, to be sexual, to be Christian.

The Anglican Theologian, R. C. Mortimer says: "Conscience is an act of practical judgment of the rightness or wrongness of a particular action. It is my reason making a moral judgment."[8]

In the last resort, each person must decide for themselves what is right and what is wrong. Human freedom demands this. We will reflect on what this means in terms of human responsibility.

To be as practical as possible, to avoid complicated language, and to shy away from theological terms, the following definition is the one found most practical. It will be the outline of this chapter's reflection, "To be Moral."

CHRISTIAN MORAL JUDGMENT

Let's be very clear about the objective of the following pages. We are going to talk about forming our conscience. I am defining conscience as making *Christian moral judgments*.

We are talking about *deciding* if something is right or wrong. I have an opportunity to make some fast money at the expense of an unsuspecting person. I have to decide. I have been invited to an art film. I have to decide. I want to go to bed with someone else's spouse. I have to decide. Should I stay in bed on Sunday morning with my headache, or go to church? I have to decide.

We are talking about a noun modified by two adjectives. The essential element, then, is *judgment*. We are going to be talking about judgment. We are going to reflect on what makes it Christian and what makes it moral so that it is a

CHRISTIAN
MORAL
JUDGMENT.

Christian

When we say this judgment is Christian, we are really saying everything we said in Chapter IV, "to be Christian." Obviously this definition is only valid for the Christian. But, that's what we are talking about. For the Christian person, the judgment will be made within the context of one's complete orientation to God. It will be Christian if Christ is in the picture. Christians find identity, find who they are, find where they are going, find what it's all about in their relationship with Christ.

In the eighth chapter of his Gospel, St. John quotes Christ as saying, "*If the Son shall set you free, then you shall be free indeed.*" Christ came as the Liberator. When the people questioned what they needed to be freed from, Jesus explained that their bondage was an inner one. St. Paul explained that they were slaves of sin, death, and the Old Law. Jesus Christ paid the price for freedom for humanity, freedom from every kind of internal slavery.

Persons who center the whole of their life on Christ become determiners of their own destiny, under Christ. The spirit is in its rightful place of dominance in the life of the person who has surrendered to Christ.

A person who is in Christ cannot disregard Christ in forming judgments of what is right or wrong. This is the primary commitment. If I make a commitment to wear clothing, I have a choice of colors, sizes, styles, etc., but I don't have a choice *not* to wear clothing. If I put on Christ, the only thing that makes any sense at all is to make all decisions according to His mind.

148

The mind of Christ can be known from the gospels. The mind of Christ can be known from the two great commandments which take the place of all the other Commandments: Love God, Love neighbor. This is the shortest summary of the New Law. If you want to know if your decision is in the mind of Christ, test it by the only standard necessary to qualify it as "Christian." Is it guided by love? Does it hurt, harm, destroy, mock, or detract from my relationship with God, or other people or both since they are almost always inseparable?

The "Christian" input into a Christian moral judgment includes a love that is a response to the boundless love of God. This will be a willing, responsive, eager love that comes from the inner depth of a grateful person.

If Christianity is a willing, voluntary, enthusiastic loyalty to Christ, that loyalty will nowhere be any more evident than in the "Christian" moral judgments of the Christian. True Christian maturity will shed a really Christian light on conscience.

Unredeemed humanity finds itself slave to the physical and emotional parts of nature. Justification bring a new attitude towards God. Regeneration begins a new kind of life *in* the soul. If there is new life, sanctification should follow.

This certainly should be marked by turning from other goals and devoting oneself exclusively to the new status as a Child of God. If this sounds heavy, it is because it is heavy truth. A Christian is changed. The presence of the Holy Spirit makes one a diftcrent person.

A person cannot be a Christian unless the moral judgments that are made reflect this new relationship with God. The in-dwelling of the Holy Spirit brings a new kind of wisdom, a new kind of power. This is a relationship that needs to be dealt with. There is a commitment that needs to be taken into consideration. There is a total orientation that makes a whole new context for all decisions.

The preceding chapter was devoted to how "to be Christian." That forms the basis for the *Christian* input into *Christian* moral judgment.

Moral

A Christian moral judgment is moral. That means it takes a lot of things into consideration. It deals with establishing principles of right and wrong, conforming to standards of right and wrong.

The word "moral" itself comes from the Latin word "mores" which means the customs, habits, manners of a people, (as the fixed customs of a people, their folkways imbued with an ethical (right and wrong) significance; customs or conventions which have the force of law.

In his book on conscience, Nelson says "about 90% of the population has no other shapers of conscience in moral matters than their parents, friends, ministers, teachers."[9]

Thus, for each individual this mental, emotional, intellectual storeroom of information and influences, standards and principles will be different.

The first standard of right and wrong is that it will conform to the Law of Love. Within that context (the primary commitment), there are thousands of other possible considerations.

The second is that it will be in line with Bible teachings. One of the main foundations of western sexual tradition is the Bible and its teaching.[10] Therefore it is important that we study the Bible, understand the Bible and follow its teachings.

Sherwin Bailey, the well known Church of England authority on "sex theology," explains that the Bible needs to be reviewed in the light of the advances in scholarship during the past century. Biblical criticism has given us a more reliable text and a better understanding of the source, structure, and purpose of the sacred writings. Recent studies have clarified and related the thought forms and abstract concepts of the Bible. We have profited from research in ancient history, comparative religion, and the Jewish background to the New Testament thought. Consequently, we can bring to the interpretation of scripture a better technical equipment, a bolder and more independent spirit of inquiry. This leads us to question and sometimes revise long established beliefs and assumptions, as well as to discover from the Bible new insights into the significance of sex in the divine purpose."

I mentioned in a preceding chapter, the Catholic study of homosexuality, headed by Father Anthony Kosnik in which it was pointed out that reinterpretation is necessary for all scripture texts traditionally used to condemn homosexuality. (And it can hardly be charged that non-homosexual scholars would make such reinterpretations for self-serving purposes).

The opinions of experts and authorities should not be ignored. Some years ago I was working in a professional Christian education situation when Pope Paul VI issued the papal letter confirming his objection to contraception. A wise priest called a congregational meeting. He and I presented a program explaining to the people how to make a Christian moral judgment in this matter. "No wise or loyal Catholic would ignore the teachings of the Pope," he said. And he proceeded to explain that this (voice of authority for them) was one of the things the people needed to take into consideration when trying to make the Christian moral judgment that would show each of them what God's will for them individually was in this matter.

We went on to discuss some of the many, many other factors that need to be weighed in this moral decision. How many children already? The health of all members of the family? The income of the family? Are there factors, such as inability to feed, clothe, care for, and educate that would make having more children irresponsible parenthood and thus immoral?

Looking at factors which may make "following the law" downright immoral is not necessarily rationalization or anarchy. Prayerfully, and with wise counsel, a person can consider alternatives for weighty reasons, can have pure motivation, and not be indulging in "rationalization" (which I presume to mean "thinking up excuses for doing evil"). Choosing the right and good and the proper for the here and now is not evil, even if some of the moral input (the law, for example) says that this "act" is evil.

Saying that abortion is always wrong is to say that in all situations where abortion would save the mother's life it cannot be performed. There are those who would say since abortion is wrong, both mother and fetus must die and the mother's reward will be great in heaven and her seven children will get along just fine without a mother.

In another book[11] I have given a contrary example. Sometimes it is necessary to follow the law even though the law seems unjust and unnecessary. I have been involved in counseling men and women imprisoned in state and federal prisons. They write to me: "I have a lover here. We want to be together the rest of our lives when we are free. I don't think God condemns a wholesome love between two people just because they are of the same sex. Physical expression is a natural, clean, good aspect of wholesome love. Therefore, we do not think it is wrong to express our love physically here in prison."

The moral input here is to take into consideration the "sitz im leben" that actually exists. The realistic fact of life in that situation is that they are in prison. They want to get out. Getting out is dependent upon following the rules of the institution. If getting out has great importance to them, it should be the "primary commitment" under which other decisions must fall in line. To break the rules, to have sex, to jeopardize their release, to compound the problems of their incarceration, is a greater evil than following a law which they consider unjust. In making the decision about what is "right" for them here and now, they have to think about where they are here and now. My counsel: follow the rules. Under those conditions, sex is immoral.

Martin Luther took a lot of things into consideration when he weighed all the "mores" that went into his Christian moral judgment that shook the very foundations of Rome. Each person has to take into account what elements of the past are to be retained and developed, what must be rejected as incompatible with the truth and facts as we now see them, what positive insights we now have, what standards, customs, principles are right for me as I seek God's will now.

Knowledge and understanding of the past can lead to sound and constructive criticism of the present. An examination of our sexual tradition will often explain why we think, act, react as we do, why sex laws are framed as they are, why certain kinds of behavior are regarded as moral or immoral.[12]

Better understanding of biological functions have changed the outlook of a lot of people, but a residue of faulty science conclusions still leaves its marks on many underlying attitudes. Part of the ancient hysterical denunciation of masturbation and homosexuality was a "semen superstition" which regarded semen as almost human, the only essential substance for new life.[13] Some ramifications of this have spilled over into trouble for heterosexuals in the "wasting of semen" in contraception.

Especially where sexual ethics are concerned, there are such long established conventions that many people take the past for granted as the rule for the future. Attitudes toward marriage, status of women, divorce, contraception, etc., are deeply rooted in the past. They reflect both the insights and wisdom and the ignorance and prejudice of former times. Being so deeply rooted, those sexual attitudes that are false and groundless are difficult to eradicate even when they have been discredited by reason or experience.[14]

The taboo against pre-marital sex in Jewish society was a good rule for the preservation of pure bloodlines which were valued highly. But in the opinion of some theologians such a restrictive rule is no longer necessary today. "Pre-marital or non-marital sex is not necessarily wrong. Properly understood and lovingly practiced, sex outside of marriage can be a good and positive part of a loving interpersonal relationship."[15] This opinion of one theologian is not given as a new rule of conduct. It is listed as an example of the kind of moral "input" that can go into making a Christian moral judgment.

Another example of change in "divine law" is the changing of the Sabbath from Saturday to Sunday. Of course there were good "reasons" for this. But that is the point. It was done and it was done for a good *reason*. Even one of the ten commandments was not considered an absolute in its application. It was changed with a change in situation.

The prohibition against eating pork, for example, was a good rule in those days when pork was almost always worm ridden.

Ancient codes, commandments, laws, rules, conventions have no *absolute* significance. They provide us with guidelines. They are subject to revision and this revision is not a denial of them and the deep insight they contain.

The moral input into Christian moral judgments includes an aesthetic sensitivity about human nature, an awareness of the universe, and a consideration of the upward and outward evolution of the person making this judgment.

When it comes to sexual moral decisions, society has given us little help in handling the matter in accordance with all the realities of our human and sexual nature and our Christian regeneration. It would seem that six of the points made by Profesor Stephen Pfurtner of the famous School of Theology at Fribourg, Switzerland would be helpful:

1. All people have a right to be happy.
2. The supreme moral commandment is: let love and reason rule.
3. Sexuality should be primarily regarded as an opportunity toward the happiness, humanizing and liberating of human life.
4. One must take the happiness of others just as much into consideration as one's own gratification. Gratification at another's expense is immoral.
5. Human sexuality is replete with psychic and functional implications for the individual and society.
6. Sexual capacity for pleasure is a human value which must be brought into harmony with the other elements of *human* life.[16]

In this book we are talking specifically about Christian *sexuality*. But the formula being explained here for making Christian moral judgments applies to all facets of life from stopping for a red traffic signal to participation in war. Whatever the area, the customs, laws, conventions of the past will enter into the data considered for the decision. From the Bible, from other valued sources, the Christian learns of moral principles and standards of conduct to apply to specific situations. But the Christian moral *judgment* is made by the individual, motivated by love for God and other people, guided by the Holy Spirit and reason. Paul Tillich says the "restatement of natural law was its formalization and its concentration into one all-embracing law, the Great Commandment — The commandment of love."[17]

This consideration of moral input can be concluded with another statement from Tillich. "One is born into a moral universe, produced by the experience of all former generations. It is a mixture of natural interest and wisdom. It gives the material in which moral decisions are made. . .to some extent we are dependent upon factual and rational authority. . .Conscience is the call of a person to be oneself."[18]

And that leads to the part that is distinctively subjective in the Christian moral judgment: the judgment itself.

Judgment

Conscience is a Christian moral judgment. This *judgment* will be a free act of a fully human being.

Before making the judgment we have looked at the matter through the rose colored glasses of "Christian" and "moral." We have considered applicable rules and standards, the general attitude of the community, and the formulations of the Judaeo-Christian ethic. We have weighed sources of information which we consider authoritative. In our particular pattern of resolving, we evaluate the facts, look at the different interpretations, consider the alternatives, and pray for the guidance of the Holy Spirit.

Now *you* have to decide. You know what you stand for. You know your basic values and principles. Your systematic evaluation (as a fully human person) will lead to a growing conviction. In all probability, you will experience no moment of blinding light in which you suddenly achieve moral certainty. Instead you can expect a gradual growing conviction, made up of insights and judgments on many different questions.

To make a fully human decision, it is necessary to search for truth, to rise above blind choice or drifting with the current of popular morality or free flowing emotion.

When it comes time for the decision "freedom and responsibility go together." If I decide upon this or that course of action regarding my conduct in sexual matters

155

(or any other matter), I am effectively using my freedom. I may make a mistake. I may need more information, deeper insight, better understanding of the situation and its probable consequences. But before I act, I must decide what is right for me and I must decide with responsibility. It may take some degree of moral courage, but a judgment must be made.[19]

Should I go to the steam bath tonight, or should I not go? As controversial as it may sound, there is no law written in heaven which says whether I should or should not go to the steam bath tonight. Nor is there an absolute answer to the question: should I go to the new Lesbian bar to cruise tonight. Nor is there a never-changing answer: should we use contraceptives this time?

When we see morality as essentially concerned with an abiding love, we will see love's imperatives as guidance into the best ways of expressing that love. Under such a conception, there will be greater or lesser goals. There will be variations in time and place and circumstances. Hence there will be variations in the possibilities of love's expression. In our decisions we shall make mistakes and even cause unintentional hurt.

But surely we would prefer that sort of world to one where we are made to think of ourselves as obedient subjects of a divine despot.[20] Father Powell pinpoints human responsibility for moral decisions in the statement: "If God pre-empted all our decisions and judgments, he would be contributing to the delinquency of minors by treating us as perpetual children.[21]

This Christian ethic says: "become the person that only you in your created freedom and by God's grace, can become.[22] For the Christian that means making choices on their own merits. Don't try to be the self that some authority (such as the church, the police force, your peer group, your parent, or the popular culture) tells you to be.

On the other hand, for the Christian, the self is not a good enough model. That's why the Christian in the process of regeneration takes on a new life and a new identification. The Christian has the Christ-model of successful human living.

−12−

When it's time to make the judgment, the Christian is aware that there is no precise mode of behavior. There is no automatic process by which one can lift out of Biblical and historical and personal mores a cut and dry answer to all the complexities that go into a decision making.

When it comes to a decision in a sexual matter, the *use* of sex in an actual life situation determines whether it is good or evil. Not all sex out of marriage is bad and not all sex within marriage is good. And this book will not get into analyzing specific sex acts for their goodness or badness. That's too easy a trap to fall into.

The formula is given clearly. Make a Christian moral judgment. Your judgment may be different from mine. But it's your judgment and your life.

Christians know that God's love and purpose will guide them in making decisions. It is their duty in life to make God's purpose actual in their concrete experience through their own decisions. And God's purpose is clear: they are to live together in love. Just how they are to do that, they must learn for themselves by trial and error, by using their heads, by keeping their eyes open, by listening to the wisdom of others *and* by recognizing that new occasions teach new duties. That is not complete absence of moral standards. On the contrary, it is putting the emphasis on the way God wills people to discover what the requirements are for us where we now are and how we now are.

A Christian moral judgment is the act of making up one's mind that one ought to do or not do this act now, or that one was right or wrong in performing this or that act then. It is one's own *reason* declaring to a person what is the here and now "will of God." In most of the decisions we make there are shades of grey, but before we act we have to decide — if we want to be fully human. Not to decide is to allow ourselves to be a victim or slave of something less than the fully human decision-making faculty that is our unique gift. "The distinctive quality of Christian ethics is that the experiences, the memories, the expectations that it brings to all phenomena are related to the experience of Jesus Christ. It finds meaning as the awareness of Christ alerts persons to the possibilities and perils of life.[23]

157

Some Comments on Christian Moral Judgment

"If it would take as long," you say, "to make a Christian moral judgment, as it has taken to wade through the above section regarding Christian moral judgment, life would be impossibly complicated." You understand this is a reflection for the general understanding of the formula.

We can never really 'get into the habit' of making decisions automatically, for this would mean surrendering some of the gifts of humanity. But it doesn't take as long to tie a shoestring as it would to teach someone how. We almost stop automatically for a red light, but if it becomes fully automatic to stop for red and go on green, sooner or later someone's going to get killed. It may be a blind person. It may be someone in an ambulance. It may be you.

Human decisions require conscious awareness, but we may not have to reflect on the whole history of Judaeo-Christian civilization to decide whether it is right or wrong for one to go to a porno movie while on vacation in a strange city while no one who knows you is looking. But *I* have to act. I have to choose. Habit isn't really enough.

As a fully human being, I cannot abdicate the decision for my actions to any other power. Mechanical beings are
not moral beings. This is the central element in the human moral character. The free decision must be made, and made responsibly.

When one has made the decision, it should be understood that this is the Will of God for me here and now. Therefore, there is a duty to obey this decision. To disobey conscience is to deliberately choose what one recognizes to be wrong and to go against what we hold to be the Will of God.

Whether it turns out to be "objectively" wrong or not, isn't the point. If you judge it wrong, it's wrong for you. I remember counselling a college student in Detroit. "I know having sex with other guys is wrong," he said, "but I have to do it. I don't use dope like my brother does, but I can't help
having sex with men." The advice: if you think it's wrong, stop it.

It is possible to reevaluate a conscience, change a judgment, but we cannot escape responsibility for following the

and it was around that time that we all lived
happily ever after

judgment as we see it now.

There are many ways a conscience can be distorted by faulty moral training. I remember an occasion when the chief of detectives in my hometown, a personal friend, called and said: "You've had some success with delinquents, I've got one for you." Darrel had been arrested for stealing from other apartments in the building where he lived. He was 17 years old and his wife, who was pregnant, was 14. After many sessions of fruitless counselling, the truth finally came out. He had no "pangs of conscience" whatsoever over stealing. It was a natural thing for him. It was the way he was brought up. His father used to take him and his younger brother on nightly expeditions with a flashlight, taking everything they could get their hands on from unlocked cars. That's not conscience. That's lack of it.

A Christian conscience, undistorted by *faulty* moral training, should be a force for peace and confidence and security. It should stimulate a person to grow in responsibility, care and commitment. Love becomes the guiding principle for all personal decisions.

I have heard people claim: "I have love in my many-successive-partners relationships. Therefore they are okay. I base all my relationships on love."

Yet, I have heard those same people speak very unlovingly of people who have a different definition of "love" — monogamous, pledged, life-long fidelity, for example. To claim to have "love" in "promiscuous" relationships and to violate love in judgmental behavior toward another person is not very convincing.

I don't want to baptize either definition in the name of the Creator, Redeemer, and Sanctifier. I do want to say that "being loving" spring from a fundamental inward reality of how a person is oriented in all inter-personal relationships.

The sense of responsibility is not given us all at once. It grows from small beginnings. The decisions made from day to day, tiny as they may seem to be, are the necessary material from which such a sense arises. As we decide on this or that particular occasion, to act as responsibly as we can, looking at the probable consequences, the direction we are taking will become clear and our later decisions will become much easier.

Conscience can offer an unwanted companion, enforcing a series of narrow prohibitions and an uneasy anxiety about violating them. Or it can be the mark of true Christian maturity. If we seem to be prisoners of society, or slaves to passion, or immobilized by indecision, our only liberation, our only way to freedom is to learn how truly to love. God's message to us in Christ is the Good News of our freedom under a new Law of Love. With this we are armed for decisions in human dignity. With these decisions we form Christian moral judgments. In Christ we know peace.

Specific Applications: Pre-packaged Answers

After the first edition of this book was published, I received several letters requesting a book which would take the principles of this book and apply them to concrete situations and give answers.

Why don't we make a list of problems and set forth the solutions?

My answer: if there is ever to be a book like that it could well be a step back into the Middle Ages. Such a book won't come from me. I couldn't write it. I don't have enough imagination.

You see, it would be impossible to apply the principles of the book and give *the* answer. It would take a 666 page book, or several of them. You'd have to think of all the possible factors that would enter into each particular problem. That would make a lot of possible answers.

Even a wise "Dear Advisor" columnist quite frequently answers a problem letter with some "ifs." "If you are telling me everything, and if I understand all the facts you've mentioned, I recommend that you get out of there fast."

But, what if there were more facts, or if the columnist misunderstands some of the facts given? Perhaps the advice would be: "Stand firm. Don't budge an inch."

Seeking advice is not wrong. It's wise. But when it comes to forming a conscience, only the person involved can make the actual decision.

Let's take something for example. Let's apply this briefly to birth control. "Dear Advice Columnist, is it right or wrong for my spouse and me to use birth control methods in our marriage?" (In the confessional it might sound something like this: "Bless me, Father, for I have sinned. After our thirteenth child, we started taking the pill.")

In order to make a Christian moral judgment, a lot of facts need to be known and weighed that have to do with that real life marriage and family.

1. Do you have children now?
   No. Yes. 2. 13.
2. Are you able to support the children you have?
   No. Yes. Almost. Comfortably. With Welfare.
3. What is your meaning of "supporting your children?"
   food, clothing
   +nice home
   +good schooling
   +college education
   +cultural opportunities
   +provisions for the future
4. Do you feel you can support more children?
5. According to which definition?
6. Do you want more children?
   No. Yes. Maybe. If. Well. . .
7. Can you take care of more children?
   Yes.
   No. I'm going crazy.
   No. I'm handicapped.
   No. I have cancer of the gizmo.
   No. I have to take care of my dying mother.
   Yes. With the help of a nurse.
   No. My husband has terminal plasticity.
8. Are there any other factors?
   Yes. Our landlord says "no children."
   Yes. I think my spouse has homosexual tendancies.

Now, if I were going to write a book of "answers" I'd have to take each possible set of combinations and say: with *this* set of circumstances, this might be the answer.

After the lengthy chapter on birth control was finished, I'd have to take one by one all the other conceivable human questions and problems. Then I could only say: this is what I think I would decide with this given information. If the data varied even a little bit in a real life application, the book's pre-packaged answer might not be valid.

In *Situation Ethics*, Fletcher says, we get the answer each time and in each situation by analyzing and weighing and judging. "There are four questions of basic and indispensable importance to be raised about every case, four factors at stake in every situation, all of which must be balanced on love's scales. *There are no foregone conclusions.*"[24]

1. The first one is the primary one. What is the purpose?
2. By what means can I achieve the purpose?
3. What is the motive?
4. What are the foreseeable consequences?

You can apply these questions to marriage and divorce, to rape and abortion, to alcohol consumption, to tobacco and marijuana. You can apply them to every "moral" decision you are faced with, the very simple ones and the ones that have a bearing on your whole life style.

These are basic and indispensable questions. But this book is suggesting Christian moral judgments that go beyond these basic questions. I suggest that everything, including love, needs to be approached in the context of "what does it really mean to be fully human and to have a primary commitment to Christ?"

Situation Ethics

In reviews of the first edition of this book, it was referred to as "situation ethics." I am not fond of labels, because they consistently run the risk of being libels. But I did rush to the library and reread Joseph Fletcher's *Situation Ethics* which I had not read since Father Kosnik assigned it for collateral reading in moral theology class.

I liked the book on the rereading. It was better than my recollection.

But 1 reject the stereotype. *Christian Sexuality* is not a situation ethics book. (I also reject any attempt to label it a process theology book, as much as I admire and concur with Father Pittenger, one its best proponents.)

I don't think I am saying exactly the same thing that Father Fletcher says in *Situation Ethics*. I don't think I use any ways near the same approach. I was, incidently, pleased to be reminded that, if indeed, I am propounding situation ethics, I am in good company with the Ṭillichs, Lehmanns, Fletchers, Brunners, Niebuhrs, and many many others.

Chapter 2, "To Be Human," is the basic premise on which the rest of this book is written. "To Be Human" goes far beyond Fletcher, in my opinion. "Love and do what thou wilt" does not say everything that *Situation Ethics* says, nor everything that *Christian Sexuality* says. Fletcher devotes his whole book to an ethical system which he says is a non-system.

I feel that Christian sexuality is more than an ethical system. It is a way of life. Christianity is life. Understanding how to be human is just as important as learning how to be moral. I have said repeatedly that they are somehow the same, that this book builds cumulatively from "To Be Human" to "To Be Sexual" to "To Be Christian" and shows how they are interrelated and inseparable.

I believe my description of a full and primary commitment to being a Christian (in chapter 4) says new and different things that *Situation Ethics* does not say. Being human, sexual, and Christian, then, are pre-requisites for being moral in the approach of this book. If I bring all the gifts and faculties of my full human-ness into the decision-making arena of my life, I will be acting in good conscience.

Responsible Sexuality

If I want my sexuality to be a Christian sexuality, then I need to make Christian moral judgments affecting my sexual fulfillment that are consistent with what it means to be human and sexual and Chrstian. The test is not: what are the rules? But: what is Christian? If we turn to the Bible, we find that the "Bible is a bundle of inconsistencies regarding sex, reflecting changing times and conditions. For example, the Old Testament approves polygamy under certain conditions, and the Apostle Paul preferred celibacy over matrimony. The churches of today would most likely regard both of these teachings as outmoded, and if this be the case with respect to polygamy and celibacy, what about premarital sex and divorce? (and homosexual love?) The plain fact of the matter is that Scripture does not consistently teach any specific laws of sexual behavior."[25]

This book has repeatedly called for more than "love and then do what you will." This is the criticism leveled by some against situation ethics. If the situation is to determine what love requires, it is terribly important how one understands the situation. . .[26] Is it merely? "We met earlier tonight and we love each other, so. . ." Ferm says a "proper regard for the situation includes an awareness of future consequences. . .dreams for the future. . .wider perspective. . ."[27]

Sex should be judged in terms of relationships and not of genital acts. "In this sense promiscuity takes on a different meaning. . .It should be defined in terms of the quality of the encounter. . ."[28]

We could go on and on. We could start the list and watch it grow. Premarital sex is okay if and if and if. . .
> homosexual love is a valid human expression if and if and if. . .
> Monogamous relationships are best but. . .
> Extramarital sex must meet these requirements. . .
> Divorce is the right thing to do when. . .

In each case we find ourselves going back to the basic foundation on which the decisions must be weigh ed and made by the individual for each situation. It doesn't do any good to say, "My cousin Lou was in a similar situation last year. She decided to. . ."

"Responsible sexuality testifies that the new life which is found in Christ will undergird the Christian approach to sex and make possible encounters based on love. God is at work in and through our relations to others. Sex can never be an end in itself, to be used and abused as people see fit. Rather, sex is always an instrument of God's love which seeks to enhance the quality of human interaction.[29]

Deane Ferm is not, by his own definition, a situation ethicist. He states that the whole point of the Christian gospel is to increase among people the love of God and people through the development of proper human relationships. He goes on to say: "Christianity teaches that fidelity is more valuable than unfaithfulness, self-respect better than self-degradation, tenderness more human than brutality, love preferable to hate. . .Any action or attitude which enhances these values. . .is good, and conversely any action or attitude which undermines them is bad."[30]

Ferm ends his excellent book with "a few norms that the church would do well to uphold. These guidelines are relevant for today and consistent with the Christian goal to increase among people the love of God and people."[31]

1. The church should continue to uphold the importance of monogamous marriage. . .and recognize that some marriages do not work, that people can lose their love for each other, and that such marriages should be dissolved.
2. The church should continue to uphold the importance and even the sanctity of the family structure.
3. The church should seek to be sensitive to young people and their sexual desires and how such desires can be creatively controlled. . . . It may be appropriate for the church to make an explicit approval of sexual intercourse for engaged couples.
4. The church should not condemn homosexuality as a disease or perversion from which all men and women need to be saved. . .and there is nothing inher ently wrong in masturbation; its ethical significance depends upon the use to which it is put.
5. The church should recognize the special situation of the single person who has sexual desires that need to be and should be fulfilled. These individuals should be taught that there is no shame to their indulgence in sex as long as it does not injure the other partner. The church should discourage extramarital sex, but not condemn every individual who finds in that a statisfactory solution to a particular problem.
6. The church should support programs of sex education.
7. The church should be a vigorous advocate of all humane forms of birth control.

8. The church should favor the removal of restrictions against obscenity and pornography, except those needed to protect the innocent and small children, although the church may disagree with some of the literature, movies, and arts. . .

Dr. Ferm concludes his book, *Responsible Sexuality*, with a statement addressed to "the church." Since most of us think of this as "the ministers," it should be translated to indicate that "we, the people of God, the church" should have this attitude toward sexuality. The translation:

The attitude of the people of God of today toward sexuality must not be couched in negative terms as has been true of the Christian people of yesterday.

"Thou shalt not" prohibitions must be replaced by the affirmation "thou shalt love."

The positive and wholesome values of sex must be stressed, but at the same time Christian people should not parrot recent trends in American society and become obsessed with sexuality. This is not the most important area of concern for the people of God, but rather one issue in a complex set of larger problems involving the human situation: violence, war, poverty, racism, and ecology [sexism, civil rights, employment, criminal justice, agism, etc., etc.]. It is the primary and prophetic purpose of the people of God to seek for the increase among people everywhere of the love of God and people.[32]

When all is said and done, "to be moral" is really only a dimension of what it is "to be Christian." At every turn, Christian moral judgments will lead one "to be Christian."

REVIEW OF CHAPTER 5

The Christian faces a hodge-podge of moral attitudes. This chapter attempts to present a systematic approach that the individual can use for deciding what is moral and immoral for him or her.

Some people think every answer can be found in rule books which determine morality by law. Historically there were such books. But many theologians consider sin to be a breaking of a right relationship with God rather than a breaking of a law.

Over the centuries, the attitude of the Christian church toward various "laws" has changed. Certainly it can be said that confusion and contradiction still reign in Christendom in the variety of attitudes toward war, poverty, racism, women's equality, birth control and abortion. Most Christian "leaders," but not all, still condemn homosexuality as automatically "sinful." But no one has the complete answer about what is sin.

Freedom to form one's conscience is better than slavery to legal codes or moral commandments.

To form one's conscience is to make a Christian moral judgment.

Conscience is a judgment (decision) that is Christian and moral.

It is Christian if it follows the mind of Christ. It is Christian if it falls in line with one's primary commitment to live and move and have one's being in Christ.

TO BE MORAL has to do with making decisions about what is right and what is wrong for me. The main thrust of this chapter is that one makes moral decisions by a careful process described as making Christian Moral Judgments. Each time I am confronted with a moral choice (should I go to this party tonight, should I tithe tomorrow?) I need to weigh all the factors involved, study it carefully in the light of what I perceive to be Christian and Moral for me under these circumstances at this time and then make a judgment which is then the will of God for me.

STUDY QUESTIONS – CHAPTER 5

OPENING EXERCISE

When the small group has gathered, they are given a challenge. Having read the chapter, they are assigned to serve as a jury to decide the guilt or innocence in the following case.

Joseph was traveling with his lover. They did not have a pact of "body fidelity" to each other. They stopped at a steam bath in a city they were passing through. Joseph met a gentleman who was everything he had always idealized. They spent the night together. Joseph did everything he could to please the Other. The Other was ever conscious of Joseph's needs and pleasure. In Joseph's mind, he was bringing all the love that was in him to this situation. He described it as the most loving, most self-giving, most satisfying, most joyful mutual exchange of love he had ever participated in. When asked if he got the Other's name and address, Joseph replied: "sometimes we are given these moments of love, just for themselves, not for the future, not for repeat, but just for the love that can be exchanged at that moment."

As the jury, you are given the above facts and the Law of Love and the principles of Chapter 5. Decide: did Joseph commit a sin, or is he innocent?

The members can present their oral arguments and the leader can take a secret or open vote. If they want to discuss it further in order to try to reach a unanimous decision, that is up to the group.

1. Do you see our system of sexual morality to be muddled and arbitrary? In what way?

2. What's wrong with rule books in morality? Does that mean there are no rules? *(To the leader: The kind of rule book referred to here is one that would label all sins and their gravity. "Premarital sex is always a sin unless . . . or only permitted if . . ."*

   This text is a rule book only in that it gives guidelines for making a Christian Moral Judgment of what is wrong or right for me in each individual decision.)

3. Some people define "sin" as "acts" one commits. Others see sin as breaking a relationship between a person and God. What is the difference between these two points of view? Which is closer to your way of looking at it? *(To the leader: an example: For years there was a person who was told that masturbation was always, under all conditions, a grave sin. He was nearly driven insane by guilt feelings for giving in to this urge occasionally during his adolescent and post adolescent years. He loved God very much and spent much time in prayer and meditation on the scriptures. Finally he was able to reach the liberating decision: I love God, God loves me, an occasional indulgence of this natural physical release does not break my love relationship with God.)*

4. The author says that morality is not a matter of majority vote. Share how you feel about holding a point of view about homosexual love that is clearly different from the majority.

5. The author says conscience is not a little voice whispering in the ear, or even the voice of God, or a feeling of guilt when we do something wrong. How do you react to these statements about what conscience is not?

6. The definition of Mortimer defines conscience as a judgment. How does this differ from the idea of voice or feeling in the previous question? *(To the leader: Judgment implies a humanly responsible decision made by the reasoning faculty of a fully human person after weighing the factors involved. "A little voice" or "feeling" strips conscience of this fully human responsible function . . . That is why it was important to understand Chapter 2, TO BE HUMAN before trying to understand this Chapter.)*

7. Deciding what is right or wrong for me is a matter of making a judgment. What does a primary commitment to Christ have to do

with making any such judgment? *(To the leader: If I am a Buddhist or anything else, I have a whole different set of moral values or moral teachings, and MOST OF ALL, I don't have the personal allegiance to the person of Jesus Christ that my commitment to Jesus Christ gives me . . .)*

8. In reference to the statistic beginning "90% . . .", who has shaped your conscience? Who should shape it? *(To the leader: wait for some answers before asking the next question.)*

   To what extent have you shaped your own conscience? *(Many homosexuals were in a state of spiritual turmoil for years because they let society form their conscience. Another example: many people in business cheat and lie, and they try to justify it on the grounds that everybody else is doing it. They too need to form their own conscience, their own Christian moral judgments and not flow with the tide of "everybody else.")*

9. What role does the opinion of experts and authorities play for you in forming your Christian Moral Judgments?

10. Are the six points quoted from Father Pfurtner a help to you in making sexual moral decisions? Which one is most meaningful to you?

11. Traditionally the Bible has been an important source of input for Christian Moral Judgments. What part does it play for you? Has the Bible helped or hindered you in forming Christian Moral Judgments about sexual behavior that you can live with?

12. "If God . . ." Comment. Do you sometimes wish God would make it easier for you by programming you for good only?

13. The author says, "When it comes to a decision in a sexual matter . . ." How do you feel about this?

14. "The free decision must be made and made responsibly, when one has made . . . will of God." Is this a new idea for you. How?

15. "The advice: . . ." If some one gave you this advice, how would you respond? If you had been this student, how would you have felt? Have you ever been in a situation where you did it and felt guilty? *(To the leader: the point here is that once a mature responsible carefully-made decision is reached, then one has a moral obligation to follow that. Many people go for years abstaining from homosexual behavior because their conscience tells them it's wrong. They should. But this does not close the door to forming a good responsible conscience which would permit homosexual behavior to this person after re-studying the data, the scriptures, all the factors involved.)*

16. Do you feel these pointers on how to form a Christian Moral Judgment will be a help to you in making good decisions about all the moral choices you are faced with?

17. Why does the author feel it is impracticable to supply a book which gives all the answers about what's right and what's wrong?

Do you agree with his explanation? Do you believe that something could be right for one person and wrong for another? Do you believe that something could be right for me in one situation and wrong in another?

18. Do you believe the "church" should do all the things Ferm suggests? Why or why not?

CONCLUDE:

1. The leader should ask if there is any confusion or question on the mind of any participant that the group might be able to clear up.

2. Give each person an opportunity to share with the others briefly what insights they have received from the chapter and from the discussion.

3. ASSIGNMENT:
   a. For the next session, the final one in a six session series, prepare a moral question for the group to discuss.
   b. For the next session choose any question from any of the five study guides that you would like to discuss.
   c. Bring to the group any question concerning sexual morality or Christian sexuality you would like to discuss.

4. Close with sentence prayer. (Giving each person an opportunity to offer a brief prayer in a sentence or two.)

6

To Be Christ-like

A LIFE OF SELF-SACRIFICING LOVE

To be Christ-like is to be:
Fully human
humanly sexual,
wholly Christian
and freely moral.

To Be Fully Human

Human beings are not a sufficient model for themselves. They are not able to lift themselves up by their own bootstraps. God entered into human life to raise humanity to a new level of consciousness. Jesus Christ gave a new dimension to human living through his human living. He said, "*I came that you might have life and have it more abundantly*." He not only gave a model for that life, living it fully, but changing it and raising it to a new level by his death and resurrection. And it is this new dimension, adoption as children of God, which makes this life fully human and makes it possible for human beings to be Christ-like. Through identification with Christ we find Him not only a model for imitation, but

173

an inner companion in whom we live and move and have our being as we live more fully the gift of life and love.

"For Christians the most important image of humanity is Jesus Christ who was incarnate in human flesh so that we might know God's intention for humanity. In Christ we see a human being able to relate to people in love, regardless of how society has defined their being or status. In Christ we also see an integration of word and deed so that love, righteousness, and obedience were lived as well as spoken. It is this lived relationship that helps to inspire men and women to join others in integrating their words and deeds of love and liberation."[1]

To Be Humanly Sexual

This new level of existence as children of God, with the glorious freedom of the children of God, gives meaning and purpose to all aspects of human life. The humanity of Jesus raised human sexuality even above the "good" that it was in creation, to an aspect of life in union with God. Jesus brought to human sexuality full realization of the meaning of "where love is, God is." The absence of love, refusal to love, is the essence of sin. Jesus Christ is the perfect pattern of authentic love. Jesus Christ, love incarnate, raises a physically sexual person to the spirit-ruled, love-dominated, fully human sexual person.

To Be Wholly Christian

is to be in Christ.

To Be Freely Moral

Is to make Christian moral judgments in the mind of Christ, with full human responsibility.

The Norm: Love as Christ Loves

The norm of the new covenant between God and the

people of God is love. A norm is something you measure things by. Christians measure, for authenticity and depth, their relationship with God and with people by the quality of their love. Therefore, this cannot be just any old love, according to just any definition. The norm is the very special self-giving love of Jesus Christ.

Christ redeems by His self-giving love. For the Christian, giving self to the other and others is a manifestation of identity with Christ's giving of Himself in His redeeming, self-sacrificing love.

A total commitment to Christ is a total commitment to love. A total commitment to love is a breaking out of bondage to self and the self idolatry of self-centeredness in order to get into the upward and outward spiral, with Christ, toward the Omega point of the fully human destiny.

Love has to do with growth. The journey to fullness of life is through the path of love. To live is to grow. The way to grow is to love after the manner of Jesus Christ.

Jesus loved to the death. The death of self is not a welcome thought for most of us. A very human Jesus prayed a very human prayer in the Garden of Gethsemane. *"If it is possible, let this cup pass from me."* The thought of dying, even to fulfill His destiny of dying for others, did not come easy even for this God-become-human. Dying to self is an inescapable Christian theme because it is the uniquely Christian way God chose for showing divine love. *"Unless the grain of wheat dies, it cannot bring forth fruit."* John 12:24 Jesus died that we might have a new and better life. A love gift from God to people with no strings attached.

Dying has life-giving potential. The enigma of dying to self to fulfill one's destiny is illustrated throughout nature in the decay of the seed to produce new fruit. The caterpillar completely gives up its wormlike identity to bring forth the beautiful soaring butterfly.

In the symbolism of water baptism by immersion, we enter with Christ into this mystery of life through death. As the waters swirl over the head and body of the immersed person, there is a drowning to the old self, a dying to the self dominated by self-love, a total surrender of the old way of being merely a physical and psychological being. The person who comes up out of this drowning death walks out alive, vibrant, with a new life principle: Jesus. The caterpillar of mere humanity has emerged to be the butterfly of a freer, more abundant destiny.

In this kind of identification with Jesus one gives up a more limited self-centered, earth hugging existence in order to be able to love and be loved more fully and effectively. One gives up (dies to) an immature clinging to self-oriented ideals in order to be able more fully to give and receive love in a wider community of love.

Christ left no doubt about what he required of a person who would claim the title of Christian. He spelled out the norm of the new covenant very explicitly. *"By this shall all people know."*

Love Unto Dying

The only course for the Christian is the course of Christ. The pattern is the self-sacrificing love of Christ who thought of others always, who gave himself until He had not another drop of blood to give.

This is, of course, the path ahead for one regenerated to a life in union with Jesus. This kind of love asks that one lay down one's life for others. Only when we do this will we be on the real path of self realization. Being determiner of one's own destiny means dying to self in order to find happiness and fulfillment in the mystery of life through death. And only by being Christ-like will one be truly a Christian.

Results of Christ-like Love

We can study Christian books, say "Christian" things, do "Christian" deeds. The test, the norm, the standard, the measure, the real way to distinguish between the genuine and the counterfit is by the quality of one's love toward others. The quality of loving is not strained, but flows freely and in

176

union with Christ.

Christ-like love seeks only the good, the fulfillment, the destiny of the one who is loved. The good news of salvation tells us: Jesus died for us because He loved us. When we find out how totally God has done away with the barrier that separated us from God, we are so grateful that all we want to do is love God and love our brothers and sisters in God's family.

Christian Sexuality

Christ-like love is essentially the gift of oneself to another and to others. Christian sexuality will then, by definition, reflect this kind of self-giving love. It is a love which moves away from self in the direction of others. This kind of love is manifested in the bedroom incidentally, in the whole of life essentially. Love gives a human meaning to sexuality. Whether that is expressed heterosexually or homosexually, its goodness depends on whether love is fully served. The truly *human* experience in sex is love. This dimension seeks fullness of life for the other through the denial of self, but aims for a mutual realization of the vision and destiny of the lovers. In unity with Jesus Christ the fully human person moves toward the Omega point of self realization using the God-given gift of Christian sexuality.

We cannot change yesterday;
    That is quite clear;
Nor begin on tomorrow,
    Until it is here.
So all this is left
    for you and me
Is to make today
    All it can be.

STUDY QUESTIONS — CHAPTER 6

Read John 15:1-8

1. Discuss John 15:1-8. Give each participant an opportunity to say what it means to him or her.
2. Refer to the assignment at the end of Chapter 5, and deal with any questions brought up.
3. What is the difference between "being Christian" and "being Christ-like"?
4. Complete the following statements in the number of words allotted.
   a. To be human is to be _____   _____
   b. To be sexual is _____   _____
   c. The most important thing about being Christian is to

   _____   _____

   d. In order to be moral it is necessary to

   _____   _____   _____   _____

   e. Christian sexuality is:

There is no single right answer. Share with the group why you completed the statements with the words you chose.

ASSIGNMENT:

Go back and re-read the book again now that you have participated in the seminar discussion sessions. You will be surprised at the things you find in print that somehow were not there before.

CONCLUDE

   a. Share with the group what changes you perceive in your thinking, your understanding, or your life since reading the book and participating in the discussions.
   b. Sentence prayer for understanding and insight and peace and joy and love for all the members of the group.

NOTES

Introduction
1. Troy Perry, *The Lord is My Shepherd and He Knows I'm Gay* (Nash, 1973), p. 63.

Chapter I
1. Arno Karlen, *Sexuality and Homosexuality* (Norton, 1971), p.XIX.
2. *Ibid.*
3. Billy Graham, "The Old Morality," *New Morality or No Morality*, Robert Campbell (Bruce, 1969), p.200.
4. *Ibid.*
5. James McCary, *Human Sexuality* (Van Nostrand, 1973), p.VII.
6. Deane Ferm, *Responsible Sexuality Now* (Seabury, 1971), p.VII.
7. Karlen, *Ibid*, p.XIX.
8. Joseph Fletcher, *Situation Ethics* (Westminster, 1966).
9. Sherwin Bailey, *Sexual Ethics: A Christian View* (MacMillan, 1966), p.57.
10. Ferm, *Op.Cit.*, p.1.
10a. Dignity is the international organization serving Gay Catholics. Its international headquarters is located at 755 Boylston Street, Boston, MA.
11. G. Rattray Taylor, *Sex in History* (Harper and Row. 1973), p.19.
12. Paul Tillich, "The Nature of a Liberating Conscience," *Conscience,* Ellis Nelson (Newman, 1973), p.69.
13. Norman Pittenger, *Love and Control in Sexuality* (Pilgrim, 1974), p.12.
13a. An excellent summary of the history of oppression is presented by my friend, Brian McNaught, in his excellent article in the *U.S. Catholic*, "The Sad Dilemma of the Gay Catholic," August, 1975.
14. Karlen, *Op.Cit.*, p.77.
15. A quarter of a million homosexuals were exterminated in Nazi gas chambers. Persecution of homosexuals began in 1934 and homosexuals were forced to wear pink triangles in the concentration camp just as Jews were forced to wear yellow stars as identification marks.
16. Karlen, *Op.Cit.*, p.XIV.
17. Rachel Wahlberg, *Jesus According to a Woman* (Paulist, 1975), p.6.
18. *Ibid.*
19. Charles Laymon, *The Interpreter's One Volume Commentary on the Bible* (Abingdon, 1971), p.806.
20. Henry Chadwick, *The Early Church* (Pelican, 1971), p.58.
21. *Ibid.*, p.59.
22. Laymon, *Op.Cit.*, p.1120.
23. *Ibid.*
24. Wahlberg, *Op.Cit.*, p.6.

25. *Ibid.*, p.7.
26. *Ibid.*, p.8.
27. *Ibid.*
28. Freda Smith, "How About Women in MCC?" *Crossroads*, (MCC San Francisco, Spring, 1973).
29. James Sandmire, "We are all One in Christ Jesus," *In Unity* (Universal Fellowship, May 1976), p.11.
30. Letty Russell, *Human Liberation in a Feminist Perspective — A Theology* (Westminster, 1974), p.20.
31. Lewis Maddocks, "The Law and the Church vs. the Homosexual," *The Same Sex*, Ralph Weltge (Pilgrim, 1969), p.94.
32. Robert Treese, "Homosexuality: A Contemporary View of the Biblical Perspective," *Loving Women/Loving Men*, Sally Gearhart and William Johnson, (Glide, 1974), p.54.
33. Howard Wells, "Critical Reflections on James H. Cone's Black Theology from a Gay Perspective," *In Unity/The Gay Christian* (Universal Fellowship, March 1976), p.37.

Chapter II
1. Richard Bach, *Jonathan Livingston Seagull*, (MacMillan, 1970).
2. Muriel James and Dorothy Jongeward, *Born To Win* (Addison-Wesley, 1973), p.96.
3. *A New Catechism* (Herder and Herder), p.8.
4. This is my terminology. The case was that of Karen Ann Quinlan in New Jersey. The State Supreme Court made the ruling in 1976.
5. *A New Catechism*, p.6.
6. Bernard Cooke, *Christian Involvement* (Argus, 1966), p.39.
7. Emil Brunner, *Our Faith* (Charles Schribner's Sons, 1962), p.36.
8. *Ibid.*, p.38.
9. *Ibid.*
10. P. D. Ouspensky, *The Psychology of Man's Possible Evolution* (Knopf, 1971), p.9.
11. *Ibid.*
12. *Ibid.*, p.11.
13. Norman Pittenger, *Love and Control In Sexuality* (Pilgrim, 1974), p.53.
14. Ouspensky, *Ibid.*
15. *Ibid.*, p.40 ff.
16. Viktor Frankl, *Man's Search for Meaning* (Washington Square, 1963), p.175.
17. *Ibid.*, p.XIV.
18. Michel Quoist, *The Meaning of Success* (Fides, 1963), p.93.
19. John Powell, *Why Am I Afraid To Tell you Who I Am?* (Argus, 1969), p.120.
20. Letty Russell, *Human Liberation from a Feminist Perspective — A Theology* (Westminister, 1974), p.33.
21. Brunner, *Op.Cit.*, p. 107.
22. Pittenger, *Op.Cit.*, p.88.
23. *Ibid.*, p.89.
24. *Ibid.*, p.36.
25. Powell, *Op.Cit.*, p.134.
26. *Ibid.*, p.34.
27. Bishop Juan Hervas, founder of Cursillos de Christiandad, author of *The Leaders Manual*.
28. John Powell, *The Secret of Staying in Love* (Argus, 1974), p.10.

29.   Brian McNaught, *Dignity National Newsletter*, June 1976.
30.   *Ibid*.
31.   Powell, *Why Am I Afraid . . .*, p.32.
32.   Gaylord Hauser, *Look Younger, Live Longer* (Fawcett, 1957), p.158.
33.   Quoist, *Op.Cit.*, p.27.
34.   Powell, *The Secret . . .*, p.56.
35.   *A New Catechism*, p.5.
36.   Pittenger, *Op.Cit.*, p.116.
37.   Quoist, *Op.Cit.*, p.33.
38.   Walter Abbott, "The Church Today," *The Documents of Vatican II* (Herder, 1966), p.214.
39.   Quoist, *Op.Cit.*, p.33.
40.   Powell, *Why Am I Afraid . . .*, p.167.
41.   Paul Tillich, "The Nature of a Liberating Conscience," *Conscience*, Ellis Nelson (Newman, 1973), p.71.
42.   Powell, *The Secret . . .*, p.74.
43.   Powell, *Why Am I Afraid . . .*, p.37.

Chapter III
1.   Kenneth and Alice Hamilton, *To Be a Man — To Be a Woman* (Abingdon, 1972), p.108.
2.   Andrew Greeley, *Sexual Intimacy* (Thomas More, 1973), p.37.
3.   James McGary, *Human Sexuality* (D. Van Nostrand, 1973), p.296.
4.   *Ibid.*, p.260.
5.   *Ibid.*, p.265.
6.   *Ibid.*, p.267.
7.   *Ibid.*, p.296.
8.   *Ibid.*, p.298.
8.   *Ibid.*, p.306.
10.   Jack Nichols, *Men's Liberation* (Penguin, 1975), p.197.
11.   Eric Berne, *Sex in Human Loving* (Pocket Books, 1971), p.182.
12.   *Ibid.*, p.183.
13.   *Ibid.*, p.184.
14.   *Ibid.*, p.195.
15.   Carl Rogers, *Carl Rogers On Encounter Groups* (Harper and Row, 1970), p.63.
16.   Deane Ferm, *Responsible Sexuality Now* (Seabury, 1971), p.32.
17.   *Ibid.*, p.36.
18.   *Ibid.*, p.37.
19.   *Ibid.*, p.38.
20.   McCary, *Op.Cit.*, p.15.
21.   *Ibid.*, p.287.
22.   *Ibid.*, p.286.
23.   John Powell, *The Secret of Staying in Love* (Argus, 1974), p.10.
24.   Greeley, *Op.Cit.*, p.37.
25.   *A New Catechism* (Herder and Herder, 1969), p.8.
26.   Greeley, *Op.Cit.*, p.45.
27.   *Ibid.*, p.65.
28.   *Ibid.*, p.64.
29.   Karla Jay and Allen Young, *After You're Out* (Links, 1975), p.9.

30. *Ibid.*, p.11.
31. McCary, *Op.Cit.*, p.146.
32. McCary, *Op.Cit.*, p.146.
33. Jay, *Op.Cit.*, p.14.
34. John Wynn, *Sexual Ethics and Christian Responsibility* (Association, 1970), p.208.
35. *Ibid.*, p.17.
36. Norman Pittenger, *Love and Control in Sexuality* (Pilgrim, 1974), p.18.
37. *Ibid.*, p.18-20.
38. Letty Russell, *Human Liberation in a Feminist Perspective — a Theology* (Westminster, 1974), p.148.
39. *Ibid.*
40. *Ibid.*
41. *Ibid.*, p.149.
42. *Ibid.*, p.151.
43. *Ibid.*, p.152.
44. *Ibid.*
45. Nichols, *Op.Cit.*, p.207.
46. *Ibid.*, p.200.
47. *Ibid.*, p.201.
48. Harvey Cox, "Sexuality and Responsibility," John Wynn, *Op.Cit.*, p.34.
49. Wynn, *Op. Cit.*, p.23.
50. Paul Lehman, "A Christian Look at the Sexual Revolution," John Wynn, *Op.Cit.*, p.78.
51. Robert Bonthius, "Sexuality as Celebration and Concern," John Wynn, *Op.Cit.*, p.161.
52. Gibson Winter, "The Outlook for an Adequate Ethic," John Wynn, *Op. Cit.*, p.47.
53. Lehman, *Op.Cit.*, p.58.
54. John L. Thomas, "The Catholic Tradition for Responsibility in Social Ethics," John Wynn, *Op. Cit.*, p.137.
55. Pittenger, *Op.Cit.*, p.16.
56. Ferm, *Op.Cit.*, p.123.
57. McCary, *Op.Cit.*, p.292.
58. McCary, *Op.Cit.*, p.352.
59. Berne, *Op.Cit.*
60. Pittenger, *Op.Cit.*, p.16.
61. Lehman, *Op.Cit.*, p.81.
62. Bonthius, *Op.Cit.*, p.166.

Chapter IV
1. Malcom Boyd, *Are You Running With Me Jesus?* (Avon, 1968).
2. *Ibid.*, p.21.
3. Michel Quoist, *The Meaning of Success* (Fides, 1963), p. 207.
4. Patricia Nell Warren is the author of two sensitive bestselling novels dealing with gay themes. *The Front Runner* and *The Fancy Dancer*.
5. Norman Pittenger, *Love and Control in Sexuality* (Pilgrim Press, 1974), p.121.
6. *Jeannine Gramick, Robert Nugent, Thomas Oddo, Homosexual Catholics, A Primer for Discussion,* (Dignity, 1975).

184

7. *Ibid.*, p.11.
8. Gregory Baum, "Catholic Homosexuals," *Commonweal,* Vol. 99, No. 19, Feb. 1974, p.481.
9. The number is increasing gradually as more and more states pass consenting adult laws.
10. Barbara Gittings, "The Homosexual and the Church," *The Same Sex,* Ralph Weltge (Pilgrim, 1969), p.148.

Chapter V
1. G. Rattray Taylor, *Sex in History* (Harper and Row, 1973), p.294.
2. *Ibid.*, p.52.
3. Norman Pittenger, *Love and Control in Sexuality* (Pilgrim, 1974), p.44.
4. *Ibid.*, p.120.
5. Nicholas Lohkamp, OFM, "A New Look at Mortal Sin," *St. Anthony Messenger,* Vol. 80:12, May 1973, p.10.
6. Paul Tillich, "The Nature of a Liberating Conscience," *Conscience,* Ellis Nelson (Newman, 1973), p.46.
7. Joseph Fletcher, *Situation Ethics* (Westminster, 1966), p.53.
8. R.C. Mortimer, "Conscience," *Conscience,* Ellis Nelson, p.123.
9. Nelson, *Conscience,* p.6.
10. John Wynn, *Sexual Ethics and Christian Responsibility* (Association, 1970), p.66.
11. Richard Mickley, *Handbook of Prison Ministry* (Universal Fellowship, 1974, revised 1976).
12. Wynn, *Op.Cit.*, p.66.
13. *Ibid.*, p.62.
14. *Ibid.*, p.8.
15. Robert Clanton, "Understanding Sex in the Age of the Pill," *New Morality or No Morality,* Campbell, p.195.
16. Stephen Pfurtner, *Commonweal,* Vol. 100, August 23, 1974, p.452.
17. Paul Tillich, *Conscience, Op. Cit.*, p.66.
18. *Ibid.*
19. Pittenger, *Op.Cit.*, p.42.
20. Roger Shinn, "Homosexuality: Christian Conviction and Inquiry," *The Same Sex,* Ralph Weltge (Pilgrim, 1969), p.48.
21. John Powell, *Why Am I Afraid to Tell You Who I Am,* (Argus, 1969), p.30.
22. Pittenger, *Op.Cit.*, p.42.
23. *Ibid.*, p.45.
24. Fletcher, *Op.Cit.*, p.127.
25. Deane Ferm, *Responsible Sexuality Now* (Seabury, 1971), p.120.
26. *Ibid.*, p.126.
27. *Ibid.*
28. *Ibid.*, p.127.
29. *Ibid.*, p.156.
30. *Ibid.*, p.158.
31. *Ibid.*, p.159.
32. *Ibid.*, p.165.

Chapter VI
1. Letty Russell, *Human Liberation in A Feminist Perspective — A Theology* (Westminster, 1974), p.65.

185

ABOUT THE BOOK

Some people are completely comfortable with the sexuality they perceive deeply imbedded in themselves. Some people are in search of a deeper understanding of themselves as human, as sexual, as Christian.

This book explores what it means to be human, to be sexual, to be Christian and offers some guidelines for making decisions that will aid in living a Christian sexuality.

"I hope you will read and understand what this book is saying."

The Rev. Elder Troy Perry,
Founder and Moderator of the Universal Fellowship
of the Metropolitan Community Churches

"This book is a 'must' for those who are striving to integrate their God-given sexuality into a pattern of consistent Christian living. I recommend it enthusiastically."

The Rev. James Sandmire,
Elder, Treasurer of the Universal Fellowship
of the Metropolitan Community Churches